Small People

Small People

How Children Develop, and What You Can Do About It

Jean Mercer

Nelson-Hall nh Chicago

Library of Congress Cataloging in Publication Data

Mercer, Jean.
    Small people.

    Bibliography: p.
    Includes index.
    1. Child development. 2. Children—Management.
I. Title.
RJ131.M37   649'.1   78-27345
ISBN 0-88229-318-4 (cloth)
ISBN 0-88229-664-7 (paper)

Manufactured in the United States of America

10   9   8   7   6   5   4   3   2   1

This book is dedicated with thanks to
Simon, Becky, Taya, William, Katie, Jeannie,
and all the children at the Treehouse
who taught me about child development

Contents

Introduction

Years ago, when I was a graduate student studying psychology, I took courses and passed exams on child development. I did well on my exams, but somewhere in the back of my mind was the lurking suspicion that what I knew had little to do with the way children actually are.

When I finally had a child of my own, my suspicions were confirmed. I did not know the answers to the simplest practical questions about child development. I did not know whether babies really cried because their diapers were wet. I did not know how soon it was "normal" to start sleeping through the night. When the doctor's receptionist criticized my letting the baby have a pacifier, I had no snappy reply based on research. And I discovered that the answers to such questions were not to be found in most books on child development, whether practical or theoretical in approach.

In those early months of motherhood, it was impossible to take time to visit the library and try to find out whether answers to my questions existed anywhere. The baby and I muddled through without benefit of expert opinion. But I could not help thinking, from time to time, how much easier it could be if I had more information at my fingertips. Even when the crises had passed, I still wondered what the answers to my questions might have been.

Because I still wondered, I decided to go through the child development research published in recent years to find the information which might really be useful to someone dealing with the day-to-day problems of a baby, a toddler, or a young elementary school child. I wanted to present information, not advice or theorizing.

No one can describe the single right way to raise children, because the right way for you depends on what you want your child to be. So much of child rearing is a matter of values. Different parents have tremendously different values with respect to their children. One child's behavior may be a source of joy to one set of parents, but a source of horror to another set. No one can give advice about values, but it is possible to give some information about the results of certain child-rearing techniques.

Children, as well as parents, are different from each other. A method which works with one child may fail with another, of different temperament and abilities. Again, no single prescription is possible, but it is possible to study how certain kinds of children respond to certain child-rearing methods. The effects of different ways of dealing with children are emphasized in this book.

The chapters that follow also stress the very basic things which young children do. Because of contraception and the small size of most American and European families today, most of us have grown up without much contact with infants or toddlers. Strict age-grading in the public schools takes away another source of contact with younger children. Modern society excludes children from adults' places and times of entertainment. As a result, many people have babies after a minimum of contact with the very young. Not surprisingly, the new parents then find that they do not know what babies act like. They have no standards of comparison. They do not know whether their baby's development is within the normal range or whether something is wrong. A nurse in their childbirth education program says all babies can sleep through the night by 2 weeks of age; their baby does not. Was the nurse wrong, or is the baby sick (or obstinate)? Because of these concerns, this book provides information about the normal variations of development.

How to Use This Book

If you want to find specific information, the index and the chapter headings will help. Some topics are covered from different points of view in several chapters, so the chapter headings alone are not enough.

Here is a brief description of the kinds of information to be found in each chapter.

Chapter 1, "The Newborn," discusses the basic needs and reflex abilities of the newborn human. The breast-feeding situation is analyzed, as are the neonate's sleeping and eating schedules. The meaning of different kinds of crying is described.

Chapter 2, "A Year of Changes," describes development between birth and one year of age. The changes which occur in a child's motor abilities are discussed, along with growth and other changes in his physical structure. Social and perceptual development in the first year and the beginnings of language conclude this chapter.

Chapter 3, "Children Have Temperaments," deals with some long-term aspects of personality aspects which may not change significantly between early childhood and adulthood. Some temperamental factors are thought to be biological in nature, while others seem to develop through relationships with other members of the child's family.

Chapter 4, "The Developing Personality," describes the emotional changes children go through as they grow. These include sleep problems, thumb-sucking, fear of strangers, and other problems which diminish with maturity, as well as more serious disorders such as hyperactivity.

Chapter 5, "Social Growth," deals with the child's relationships with other people, whether in the family or in a day-care setting. The social processes of becoming toilet trained and of developing a moral code are also described in this chapter.

Chapter 6, "The Growing Mind," is about the child's ways of looking at the world. Language development and the process of getting ready to read are also described here. This chapter also discusses how parents can decide whether their children are receiving enough stimulation at home.

Chapter 7, "Physical Growth and Abilities," discusses growth in size and changes in physical shape and posture. The development of physical skills is based partly on these changes and partly on the child's experiences.

Chapter 8, "Socializing the Child," describes techniques which parents can use to change a child's behavior. Behavior modification techniques are discussed in detail.

Where to Find More Information

This book is an attempt to present a great deal of research in an abbreviated form. The reader may want to know more about some of the studies which are mentioned, or to find out whether more information has been published since this book was written. If you live in an area where you have access to a good college, university, or medical library, it will not be difficult to find more information through the following sources.

Bibliographies, whether in this or in other books on child development, can be used to find the original material. In this book, wherever a piece of research is discussed, you will find the author's name and the date of publication in parentheses. In some books, you will find a number in parentheses after a reference to a piece of research. At the end of the book, or, in some books, at the end of the chapter, you will find a bibliography which presents the works referred to in alphabetical order *or* according to number. If the work in question is a book, you will have no problem with the reference. Journal or magazine articles are more tricky. To save tears in the library, be sure to note the volume number (usually italicized). If the journal's name is abbreviated and unfamiliar to you, ask a reference librarian for help. The librarian will remember, even if you can't, that *J. Gen. Psychol.* means *Journal of General Psychology,* not *Journal of Genetic Psychology* (which is *J. Genet. Psychol.*).

Reading the article may seem very heavy going if you are not used to the style of scientific journals. Remember that almost every journal requires its articles to have summaries, which may be placed either at the beginning or at the end of the article. Read the summary first, and you will get much more out of the article. There is usually a section called "Discussion" or "Results and discussion," which may be quite useful even if you do not understand other parts of the article.

Psychological abstracts give brief summaries of most articles published on child development. Even if the original articles are not available to you, you can gain some information from these summaries. If you are not familiar with these volumes, you could save a lot of frustration by asking a reference librarian to show you how to use them.

Fads in Child Rearing

Just as hemlines change and car styles vary from year to year, child-care techniques have their fashions. Thirty-five years ago, in the heyday of behaviorism, babies were never to be cuddled or picked up when they cried; they were to be fed every four hours and no more often; they were not to be taken into their parents' beds. Five years ago, in some circles, babies were to be breast-fed as often as they liked until they weaned themselves; they were not to be pressured or even encouraged about toilet training; they were to be carried and cuddled by their parents everywhere. And the children survived both regimes. We would do well to learn from this that no loudly heralded new method is actually the great new discovery in child rearing, but that any set of routines which suits both parents and children is perfectly all right. Children have a powerful drive to grow and mature, and no single little mistake made by a parent ever "ruined" a child. So this book does not tell you "how to do it"; but it is to be hoped that each reader can gain from new knowledge some confidence in his or her own ways.

Apology for the Use of "He"

Many child development books today stress the use of "she" as well as "he" to refer to babies and children. I suppose it is because my only child is a boy that I usually think of babies as "he." I have used "he" in this book whenever I was not talking specifically about girls. I hope that this will not offend anyone, and that the frequent references to sex differences will indicate that the development of girls is very important too.

Chapter 1
The Newborn

Newborn babies react to the world by a series of reflexes, before they
have learned any voluntary behavior. The tendency to suck is a strong
and vital reflex. All of the newborn's sensory systems are functioning,
but their visual abilities are not as good as those of adults, and they are
relatively insensitive to pain. The nervous system is quite immature. Eating and sleeping occur at frequent intervals. Crying is the most important form of communication, and it follows predictable patterns, depending on its cause.

A newborn baby seems "new" because he can now be seen by
his parents for the first time. His mother has been aware of his
presence and his movements for four or five months, but of course
could only guess at important details like sex, size, and possession
of hair. But the baby's apparent newness is deceptive. He has actually had nine months of growth and experience, culminating in
the long, uncomfortable, and rather dangerous trip through the
four inches of the birth canal. He shows the impact of his environment: his growth has been determined by his mother's health and
nutrition, and his behavior may be affected by her serenity or agi-

1

tation during his prenatal life. The birth experience, too, may determine for good or ill the baby's capacity to deal with the world. A birth which is too fast or too slow, one which bruises the infant's head against the maternal pelvis or the forceps, or one which shocks him by the suddenness of Caesarean section may leave him permanently damaged. Someone who has already experienced so much danger and adventure is "new" only from the point of view of those who must now begin actively to care for him.

The newly born person is usually thought of as helpless and unable to respond to his environment. In the past, it was even believed that he could not see or hear. Certainly, the neonate's capacities are very different from those of the adult. But it is clear that he does respond to the world and that he can act on it in some essential ways. The infant's abilities are best shown in his *reflex* responses to stimulation, in his development of *sucking* skill, and in his *auditory and visual perception.*

Reflexes: What the Newborn Can Do and How to See Him Doing It

A reflex is an action which is involuntary, which has not been learned, and which occurs simply because of the way the nervous system is put together. Reflexes occur in response to very specific kinds of stimulation. Most adults have observed their own knee-jerk reflex, which can be seen during a medical examination when the doctor taps just below the kneecap with his reflex hammer. Looking at other people, it is easy to see pupillary reflexes, which cause the pupil of the eye to contract in bright light and to expand when the light is dim.

The newborn baby shares some reflexes, like the pupillary reflex, with adults, but he also has some reflexes which are not seen in older people. Some of these reactions, in fact, disappear in the first few days of life. Others will be gone in a few months, never to be seen again as long as the individual remains in good health.

One reflex which passes away very quickly is the *doll's-eye reflex,* which disappears in a day or so after birth. If the baby is supported on someone's hands and tilted back and forth, so that his position alternates between lying down and "standing" upright, his eyes will roll up and down in his head like those of a doll with moving eyes.

Figure 1.
Modification of the Moro reflex as the baby matures.

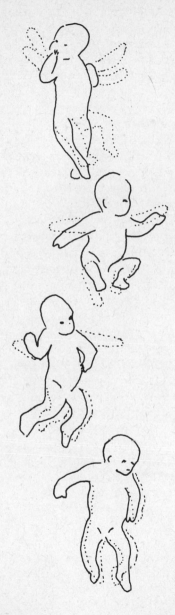

The *Babinski reflex* is produced by running a finger up the sole of the infant's foot. In response to this stimulation, his toes all fan upward. (He may also withdraw the foot.) Later in life, a healthy child or adult will respond to such tickling by curling all the toes down toward the sole of the foot.

The newborn has a startlingly powerful *grasp reflex*. He will grip anything that touches the palm of his hand, and when the mother uncurls his fingers to wash them she often finds pieces of cotton or paper or strands of her own hair. The fists are clenched most of the time. (Where we would say someone sleeps "like a baby," the French say that he sleeps "with clenched fists"—a nice allusion to the newborn's favorite hand position.) This reflex is not only frequent in occurrence, but very strong. The newborn infant can actually support his own weight if you give him two fingers to grasp and then lift him.

The *Moro or startle reflex* is a disturbing one for new parents. This reflex occurs when the baby is held with his back down and lowered. The reflex action consists of drawing up the legs and flinging out the arms very suddenly. It is often accompanied by crying and in some babies seems to occur whenever they are laid down for diapering, no matter how gentle the parent tries to be. When the Moro reflex is extreme and frequent in occurrence, it may be quite distressing to the parents, since it seems that nothing they can do is enough to keep the baby from getting upset. In fact, however, this reflex, like many of the reflex reactions of the newborn, will become modified and pass away after a while. Figure 1 shows how the Moro reflex gradually becomes reduced to a slight jump of surprise.

The *swimming reflex* occurs when the baby is held tummy down in water and consists of swimming movements, as Figure 2 shows. This reflex, which would be useful for everyone to keep, disappears within the first year of life.

The newborn baby shows a *stepping reflex* which is similar to the movements of walking. When he is held upright with his feet pressed against a flat surface, he will reflexively move his feet (although he cannot support much of his weight with his legs, of course). In ordinary circumstances, this reflex disappears like the others. However, there now seems to be some evidence that con-

Figure 2.
The swimming reflex.

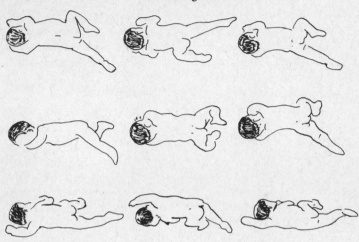

tinued practice will maintain the reflex. Children whose parents frequently hold them upright, with their feet on a surface, will continue to show the stepping reflex and in fact will walk at an unusually early age.

One of the neonate's reflexes can serve to predict with some accuracy whether he will later be right- or left-handed. The *tonic neck reflex,* shown in Figure 3, appears when the child is lying on his back. The head is turned to the right or left. If the head is facing right, the right arm and leg are extended and the left leg and arm are flexed, while the opposite is true if the head faces left.

The *rooting* and *sucking* reflexes are essential for survival and are relevant to our next topic, the development of the infant's sucking ability. In the rooting reflex, any pressure or touch on the cheek causes the baby to move its face toward that side. This helps the baby find the nipple when it is held up to the breast. (It also can cause problems when one carries a baby with its face against one's neck. The baby reflexively pushes against the neck. The adult pushes back in order to get into a more comfortable position, whereupon the rooting reflex is more strongly activated and the baby pushes back even harder. The thing to do is to move one's head away from the baby, resettle him, and then move the head back.) The sucking reflex refers simply to the baby's built-in tendency to suck on anything which comes to his mouth. The strength of this reflex depends on the baby's hunger and his general state of health and development. The effects of sedation of the mother during childbirth may reduce the baby's sucking rate for at least four days.

Figure 3.
The tonic neck reflex.

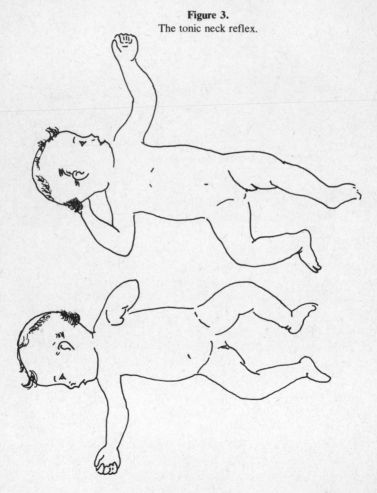

Sucking and Learning

An infant's sucking is a complicated matter, depending partly on his own state and partly on the material which is offered to him to suck. It is also an essential matter for, although some babies have been maintained from birth on cup feeding, most are offered their nourishment from the breast or from a bottle.

An important point to remember when we consider sucking is that a baby must suck differently in order to get milk from a bottle than he does in order to get milk from the breast. In sucking from a bottle, the baby lowers the pressure in his mouth so that the milk flows in passively, much as an older child does when drinking through a straw.

Sucking from the breast, on the other hand, involves a coordination of two sets of reflexes: those of the infant and those of the mother. The pressure of the infant's mouth on the nipple causes the breast actively to squirt a stream of milk into the mouth. (Mothers who have breast-fed their babies or who have expressed milk from their breasts by hand know that appropriate pressure just behind the nipple can squirt milk as far as three feet.) The baby must exert the pressure of its jaws in a sort of chewing movement, and the nipple must be inserted well into the mouth in order for the pressure to "pinch" the breast tissues in the right way and cause milk to be expelled.

One of the first things learned by a newborn baby is how to adapt its reflexive sucking movements to conform to the bottle or the breast. This learning quickly becomes consolidated, so that it is very difficult for a breast-fed baby to change to a bottle, or vice versa. This is why weaning a baby from breast to bottle can be very difficult if the baby has never had a bottle before. A mother who is planning to wean from breast to bottle rather than breast to cup will do well to give an occasional bottle from an early age so the baby will learn how to perform both kinds of sucking. The infant who does not wean to the bottle easily is not simply being stubborn or "conservative"; he actually does not know how to suck from the bottle.

The establishment of expertise in sucking from the breast depends to some extent on the shape of the mother's nipple and the surrounding breast tissues. The tissues need to be very soft and yielding, so that the nipple can be pulled forward and the pressure of the baby's jaws comes behind the nipple itself. (A baby chewing on the nipple will get no milk, and the mother will be very uncomfortable after a while.) One pregnancy is sometimes not sufficient to get the breast tissues into the necessary shape, but two pregnancies will usually do the trick (according to Mavis Gunther, 1970). Gunther remarks on "the extraordinary apathy of a baby if it is put to the breast but does not get the whole feeling in its mouth. If it has not got the right pattern of the stimulus on its soft palate, tongue, and oral cavity, it will stay apathetic"—in spite of increasing hunger (1970, p. 38).

.When the breast is poorly shaped or too full of milk, the baby's nose may be blocked when it takes the nipple in its mouth. In this case, the reflexive tendency to withdraw from a suffocating object wins out over the reflexive tendency to suck, and the baby fights the breast by pushing away with its fists. After a few such experiences, the baby will cry and fight as soon as it is picked up and turned toward the mother. As Gunther puts it, "generally speaking this is a situation which no mother can endure. It is literally frightful for the mother. Mothers who have endured it lose all wish to feed the baby because they cannot bear being so rejected by the baby" (1970, p. 38).

Seeing, Hearing, and Feeling

Not too many years ago, it was widely believed that newborn babies could not see or hear. This attitude is still held by some parents (and one even occasionally encounters prospective mothers who believe that their baby will be born with eyes closed, like a puppy!). In fact, more recent research shows clearly that the neonate has effective vision and audition, though he does not see or hear as well as an adult does.

Babies between birth and 1 month are very nearsighted. That is, they have good vision for near objects but do not see distant things very clearly. A baby may be able to see at a distance of 20 feet an object which a normal adult could see at 400 feet. The newborn infant has poor accommodation (the ability to see clearly at a distance and then switch to clear vision nearby). They see best objects which are about 8 inches away—for instance, the mother's face when the baby is at the breast. Color vision is certainly present, but it is difficult to measure whether the infant discriminates colors as well as adults to (Pick and Pick, 1970).

Babies do not seem to prefer one color over others, according to some research (Kessen, et al., 1970).

It is not very clear whether newborn infants can detect very soft sounds, but at one to four days of age they can apparently hear sounds as loud as normal conversation (Pick, in Mussen's Carmichael, 1970). Babies are soothed and helped to sleep not by absolute silence but by the presence of "white noise"—a mixture of frequencies, like the hum produced by an electric fan. Hearing the rhythm of a heartbeat, which is popularly thought to be soothing to infants, does not seem to make any difference to factors like weight gain (Palmgrist, 1975). Newborn babies are especially sensitive to the human voice and it has been shown that they move in the same rhythm as speech they are hearing at any point, though they do not coordinate their movements with tapping or disconnected vowel sounds (Condon and Sander, 1974). This suggests that from the day of birth infants are learning about the rhythmic sound patterns of the language which will be theirs, and that talking to neonates may well be a valuable form of teaching.

Young babies are sensitive to differences in smell and taste. Unpleasant odors, like those of some medicines, may cause the baby to refuse to take the breast. Sweet tastes are preferred and salty, sour, and bitter tastes are rejected.

The sense of pain is not strongly developed in the newborn. Babies are circumcised without an anesthetic and without showing much change in heart rate. In fact, external sources of discomfort do not seem very important to the neonate. Even wet diapers, so often blamed as a cause of crying, do not seem to bother the infant much; if you pin the same wet diapers back on him, he is just as likely to stop crying as if you gave him dry ones (Wolff, 1970).

How the Brain Grows and Develops

All that the newborn child can see, hear, feel, or do depends on the state of development of his nervous system. The months before birth and the first 6 years of postnatal life are the times when the nervous system is developing at a rate far beyond anything which it will ever experience again. Figure 4 gives an idea of the tremendous growth of the brain and head early in life. The brain reaches adult size and complexity before any other body part does (see Figure 5 for a comparison of the brains of a four-month fetus and a full-term baby).

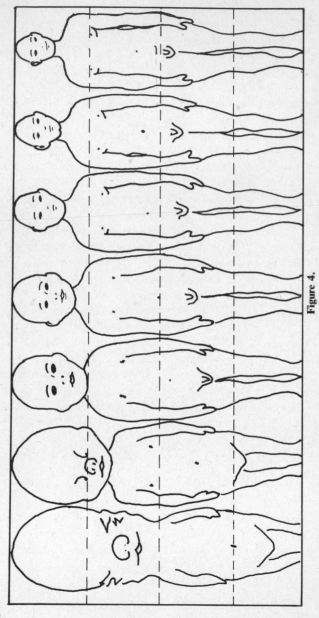

Figure 4.

Change in relative size of head with maturation. (From C. M. Jackson, "Some Aspects of Form and Growth," in Robbins, Hogan, Jackson, and Green (eds.), *Growth*, p. 118. Used with permission of Yale University Press.)

Figure 5.
The brain of a four-month fetus compared to that of a full-term baby.

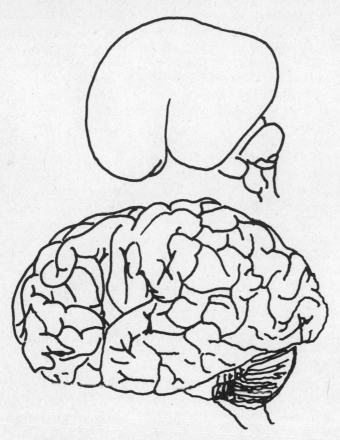

The large size of the baby's head determines, to some extent, the time when human babies must be born. The head is the largest part of the infant; if the head is born successfully, the rest of the baby is bound to be able to follow. If human pregnancy lasted any longer than it does, it would be impossible for the infant's larger head to pass through the bones of the mother's pelvis. One result of this is that human babies are born at a state of considerably less maturity than the young of other species. They thus require much more constant, careful, and long-term care than do animal babies. This may be seen as something of a nuisance from the viewpoints of parents and teachers, since the immaturity of babies and children makes them very demanding. But the long immaturity of humans is probably also the key to the development of human culture and language, for the essential close contact between infants and adults gives the time and opportunity for the adults to pass on their experience, knowledge, and values to the young ones.

The rapidity of brain growth during early development makes it crucial that the growing individual have sufficient protein. Nervous system tissue is more sensitive than the rest of the body to a lack of protein, and insufficient nutrition during the early stages of development may permanently damage the brain. The prenatal period, infancy, and early childhood are critical periods for brain development. If circumstances during this time prevent the nervous system from growing normally, no amount of treatment in later life can ever undo the damage. The nervous system must develop when it is time for it to develop, or it does not develop at all. Thus, famine in a country produces more than immediate death of the starved children: it may guarantee a generation of abnormal, retarded individuals who survived the famine physically but not neurologically.

If the brain is so sensitive at this stage of development, why is it not more frequently damaged by the pressures of birth or by falls on the head? In fact, the brain is very well protected from external pressures. The skull, the outermost layer of protective material, is of course incomplete at birth and is molded gradually by the pressures of labor into a shape which can pass through the vagina. The brain is also covered by tough, thick membranes and by a layer of fluid which cushions it against blows or pressure. The fontanel (the "soft spot" or incomplete part of the baby's skull at birth) may remain open until eighteen months of age or later without danger, since the internal protection of the brain is so effective. In fact, the caution most people feel about touching the fontanel is unnecessary, and it is rather interesting to feel it from time to time in order to check on the progress being made in the growth of an infant's skull. The brain at this age is also very soft and malleable. However, the brain and spinal cord are very susceptible to whiplash injury, and a baby or toddler should never be punished by shaking.

In fact, the greatest danger to the development of an infant's brain is internal, not external. Certain infections, especially those which cause high fevers, and the lack of protein or of oxygen are the major sources of damage to the developing nervous system. Lack of oxygen is most likely to occur during a difficult delivery.

Occasionally a mother is warned off breast-feeding by her doctor, with the comment that it may cause the child's brain to be damaged. This sounds farfetched, but it may temporarily be true. The relationship between the mother's milk and brain damage is a complex one. Babies before birth have a larger supply of red blood cells than they need after they are born and begin to breathe. After birth, the extra red blood cells are broken down and disposed of by the liver. Unfortunately, the newborn baby's liver is not as efficient as it will later be, and it does not always manage to break down the red blood cells completely. When this occurs, a side product of the cells may be bilirubin, a toxic pigment to which the brain is very sensitive. Bilirubin also makes the skin yellowish, producing neonatal jaundice. Now, where does the mother's milk come into this? During pregnancy, the mother's body produced more than its normal amount of the sex hormone estrogen. After birth, the excess estrogen is excreted, and one of the means of excretion is the milk. The nursing baby thus receives a heavy dose of estrogen in the first week of life. Estrogen can function to depress still further the efficiency of the newborn liver, which causes the bilirubin level to become higher and the jaundice to get worse. This is a serious consideration, since exposure of the brain to very high bilirubin levels for too long may result in deafness and odd involuntary movements of the hands and arms. (However, it should be noted that most of the estrogen has been excreted by a week after birth, and breast-feeding may be established then.)

The infant's brain is not simply growing in size. Its cells are changing individually and developing new connections with each other, making possible new behaviors and new sensory abilities.

The most obvious change in the cells of the nervous system is myelination. Some brain cells are coated with a white fatty substance called myelin, while others are not. The myelinated cells are more efficient and faster in their reactions. At birth, few of the cells of the cortex (the part of the brain most important for perception, consciousness, and voluntary movement) have developed their myelin coating. At this stage, the cortex does not function effectively. But soon, if the infant's diet is good, myelination proceeds and the cortex begins to "wake up." The development of the cortex is shown in behavior, as the infant begins to become more alert and to look carefully at his surroundings. The loss of the reflexes which are present at birth also shows the development of the cortex, as voluntary activity begins to replace involuntary reflex actions.

An important aspect of brain development in the newborn has to do with experience. We cannot test these things directly in human beings, of course, but research on baby animals shows that if the individual is reared in the dark, there is little or no development of the parts of the cortex which have to do with vision. Visual experience is needed before brain development can progress to completion. Again, as with the need for protein, there is probably a critical period when some visual stimulation is essential if normal vision is ever going to exist. This does not mean that a baby should always be in a brightly lit room with lots of color and pattern, but it does seem clear that babies who have interesting things to look at develop their looking skills faster than those who do not. (There are some babies who seem upset by colorful objects in the early weeks, however.)

Eating and Sleeping

The immaturity of the newborn infant is revealed by his polyphasia. He eats and sleeps at many short intervals throughout the day and night, rather than in a few distinct meals and one long night sleep like those of adults. The change from polyphasia to a more adultlike pattern occurs as a result of development, not learning; tired as they may be, the parents of the newborn must wait for him to become capable of sleeping through the night. All of the baby's physiological processes are faster than those of adults. His heart and breathing rates are about twice as fast as those of adults, and he urinates about eighteen times and defecates four to seven times in twenty-four hours (Landreth, 1967).

The four-hour feeding schedule, once so dear to the hearts of American parents and pediatricians, was apparently derived from one very brief and dubious piece of research. "The four-hour schedule of feeding apparently originated with a barium x-ray study of three newborns in 1900 which showed that the stomach emptied after about four hours. The generalization from three newborns fed a foreign substance to milk-drinking infants in general is, at best, dubious" (Kessen et al., 1970, p. 332).

Figure 6.

How one hundred infants regulated their feedings. (From C. A. Aldrich and E. S. Hewitt, "A Self-regulating Feeding Program for Infants," *Journal of the American Medical Association,* 1947, *135,* pp. 340-42. Copyright © 1947, American Medical Association.)

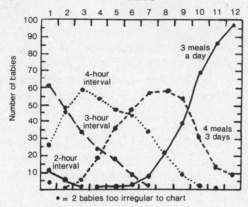

As Figure 6 shows, most babies who are fed on demand begin life preferring to eat every two or three hours rather than every 4 hours. They gradually become able to take more food at a time and eat at longer and longer intervals.

The preference of the newborn baby for meals every two or three hours jibes with the needs of the nursing mother. Milk production in the mother needs to be built up in order to match the appetite of the infant. The more milk the baby takes, and the more frequently suckling occurs, the more milk the mother will produce. A two- or three-hour nursing schedule works very well for building up the milk production of most women, whereas a four-hour schedule may be too infrequent at the beginning. The days of the four-hour feeding schedule were also the days in which many women "could not" nurse their babies. Women who "just didn't have enough milk" were accused of being neurotic, or nervous, or uncomfortable with their femininity, when in fact the real problem was probably that they were not putting the baby to the breast often enough.

The newborn baby sleeps a great deal, an average of seventeen hours a day in the first three days of life (Parmelee, quoted in Landreth, 1967). It has been suggested that the newborn experiences only "wakefulness of necessity"—it awakens only when disturbed by the need for food or elimination. It may be that only the development of the cortex allows the infant to have a true variation between being "wide awake" and "deeply asleep."

Crying

Anyone who has been with young babies recognizes that they cry a good deal and that their cry is very difficult to ignore. Only a folk song would be so unrealistic as to declare that someone "gave my love a baby with no cryin'." The average amount of crying per day at six weeks of age is 2.75 hours (Brazelton, 1962).

One student of crying (Wolff, 1970) has described four different patterns of newborn crying, each with some relation to a particular cause of crying. The hunger cry is usually heard when the baby is hungry, but has other causes too. It consists of a cry (about 0.6 second in duration), followed by a short silence (about 0.2 second), a whistling inhalation (0.1 to 0.2 second), another brief pause, and another cry. Table 1 shows this pattern.

The angry cry of the newborn follows the same pattern as the hunger cry, but it has a different tonal quality because of the turbulence of excess air being forced through the vocal cords. Table 2 describes the angry cry.

The newborn's pain cry is very noticeably different from the other two cries described above. The pain begins with a long cry, followed by a long pause of complete silence and inactivity, then a gasp of inhalation followed by more cries. "The subjective features which distinguish the pain cry from other patterns are: (1) a sudden onset of loud crying without preliminary moaning, (2) the initial long cry, and (3) the extended period of breath-holding in

Table 1
The rhythmical cry of a 4-day-old infant

Cry Proper	Rest	Inspiration	Rest
• 63 secs	• 08 secs	• 03 secs	• 17 secs
• 62	• 05	• 03	• 15
• 70	• 06	• 04	• 26
• 51	• 08	• 03	• 15
• 87	• 10	—	—
• 24	• 05	—	—
• 64	• 02	• 04	• 17
—	—	• 04	• 28
• 57	• 04	• 04	• 17
• 64	• 03	• 03	• 27
• 70	• 09	• 04	• 09
• 64	• 16	• 04	• 14
• 64	(?)	• 05	• 24
• 61	• 24	• 04	• 24
• 79	• 09	• 04	• 21
• 59	• 10	• 04	• 19
• 56	• 09	• 05	• 19
• 06	—	—	—

Table 2
The "mad" cry of a 3-day-old infant

Cry Proper	Rest	Inspiration	Rest
• 78 secs	• 18 secs	• 04 secs	• 17 secs
• 69	• 15	• 04	• 15
• 69	• 19	• 04	• 24
• 77	• 21	• 06	• 15
• 74	• 23	• 04	• 14
• 68	• 24	• 04	• 11
• 65	• 29	—	—
• 60	• 27	• 04	• 06
• 70	• 30	• 06	• 09
• 62	• 23	• 06	• 11
• 62	• 30	• 07	• 02
• 62	• 18	• 10	• 06
		• 06	• 09
		• 08	• 04
• 09	• 15	• 03	• 04
		• 04	• 12
• 62	• 09	• 03	• 15
• 76	• 21	• 06	• 12
• 67	• 06	• 03	• 15
• 67	• 04	• 03	• 12
• 61	• 24	• 03	• 09

(From P. H. Wolff, "The Natural History of Crying and Other Vocalizations in Early Infancy," in B. Foss (ed.), *Determinants of Infant Behavior,* Vol. IV, London: Methuen, 1970; p. 83.)

Table 3
Crying in response to physical pain

Cry Proper	Rest	Inspiration	Rest
4 • 10	7 • 20	• 27	• 10
3 • 56	• 78	• 09	• 23
1 • 98	• 48	—	—
1 • 02	• 47	• 04	• 15
• 78	• 39	• 10	• 37
• 70	• 05	• 12	• 23
• 64	• 08	• 06	—

(From P. H. Wolff, "The Natural History of Crying and Other Vocalizations in Early Infancy," in B. Foss (ed.), *Determinants of Infant Behavior,* Vol. IV, London: Methuen, 1970, p. 85.)

expiration after the long cry. The 'natural unit' which one hears when there is more than one long pain cry, consists of an inspiratory whistle immediately followed by a long expiratory cry rather than a cry followed by an inspiration" (Wolff, p. 85). Table 3 describes this cry. The pain cry is very closely associated with injury. If no pain cry has been heard, it is very unlikely that an infant's crying is caused by an open diaper pin or other obvious source of pain.

The fourth variation on the cry is frustration crying, which arises, for instance, if the baby is happily sucking on a pacifier and the pacifier is pulled out of his mouth. The first cries "are long and drawn out (three to five seconds), and like the pain cry they start from a condition of complete silence. But since there is no prolonged breath-holding after the initial cries, and the inspiratory whistle follows shortly after the expiration, one hears the 'natural unit' as a cry followed by an inspiratory whistle rather than as an inspiration followed by a cry. This gives the listener a rather different subjective impression than does the pain or hunger cry" (Wolff, pp. 85-86). Figure 9 illustrates the frustration cry.

What, other than feeding, gets babies to stop crying? Wolff found that some effective methods of soothing the crying infant were picking him up, tapping him rhythmically on the back, and swaddling him so that his limbs are immobilized. For some babies, pressing the flat of the hand on the chest or abdomen was helpful.

Two common causes of crying are cold and lack of physical contact with a person or with clothing. Babies cry more and sleep

Table 4
Cry in response to removal of pacifier

Cry Proper	Rest	Inspiration	Rest
3 · 21	· 06	· 06	· 29
1 · 46	· 06	—	—
· 93	· 03	· 09	· 27
· 87	· 04	· 07	· 23
1 · 38	· 04	· 09	· 12
· 80	· 04	· 10	· 18
· 67	· 05	· 15	· 10

(From P. H. Wolff, "The Natural History of Crying and Other Vocalizations in Early Infancy," in B. Foss (ed.), *Determinants of Infant Behavior*, Vol. IV, London: Methuen, 1970, p. 86.)

less in a cool than a warm environment, although some also object vociferously to being too hot. Even when kept warm enough, some young babies object to having their clothes taken off, and stop crying when the chest and abdomen are covered with a soft cloth. Rocking is the most consistent soother up to three months (Kopp, 1971).

Pacifier sucking is one of the most effective protectors of sleep and preventers of crying. A baby who is not sucking shows a lot of diffuse motor activity, and he may jerk or twitch in his sleep and wake himself up, leading to long protest against being awakened. The pacifier prevents crying and thrashing by preventing the infant from being rudely awakened by jerking.

Testing the Status of the Newborn

Not all babies are at the same stage of development when they are born. Obviously, the premature baby has come into the world with one or two fewer months of development than his full-term brother. Other factors help make one baby act differently at birth from another. Lack of oxygen, bruising from forceps or a difficult delivery, and anaesthesia of the mother all affect the state of the child. Hospitals now commonly test each baby's state at one and at five minutes after birth and assign him an Apgar score (Apgar, 1953, in Landreth). The Apgar score is based on the rating of heart rate, respiratory efficiency, reflex irritability, muscle tone, and color. Each of these may receive a score from 0 to 2, and a "perfect" score is 10. For instance, a child who does not breathe

Table 5
The Apgar scale

Apgar score

Sign	0	1	2
Heart rate	absent	slow (below 100)	rapid (over 100)
Respiratory effort	absent	irregular, slow	good, crying
Muscle tone	flaccid, limp	weak, inactive	strong, active
Color	blue, pale	body pink, extremities blue	entirely pink
Reflex irritability	no response	grimace	coughing, sneezing, crying

Each sign is rated in terms of absence or presence from 0 to 2; highest overall score is 10.
(From *A Child's World: Infancy through Adolescence* by D. Papalia and S. Olds, p. 104. Copyright © 1975. Used with permission of McGraw-Hill Book Company.)

for sixty seconds scores 0, and one who cries loudly right away scores 2 on respiratory efficiency.

A behavioral assessment, developed by Graham (1956, in Landreth) and Rosenblith (1974), is less frequently used. It involves ratings on aspects such as (1) the infant's head reaction when he is placed prone, (2) crawling reactions when the infant is prone, (3) responses to a piece of cotton over the nose, (4) responses to a piece of cellophane over nose and mouth, (5) vigor of responses, and (6) strength of the grasp reflex.

These tests are useful in determining which infants needs special care, but they are not strongly related to measures of intelligence or abilities when the child is much older. A poor score is more likely to predict poor ability in later life than a good score is to predict good ability.

Chapter 2
A Year of Changes

The growth of physical abilities follows an almost invariable sequence of motor milestones. Growth is rapid at first and later slows. Physical proportions change, so that the lower part of the body becomes proportionately bigger than it was at birth. Girls' physical maturity is advanced over boys', though they are about the same size. Social development involves smiling by the age of six weeks or so. Later, fear of strangers develops. Perceptual changes occur, improving vision and allowing for a better interpretation of the world.

A Crucial Year

No other year in the child's life will be as important as this first one. His experiences and his nutrition during this time are essential determinants of the person he will be in the future. Ashley Montagu has even applied to the first year of life the concept of "exterogestation"—the idea that the immature body and brain must be nourished by food and proper treatment in order to develop after birth, just as they had to be nourished in the prenatal environment.

The Direction of Development

Babies and children do not always do things at exactly the same ages as their brothers and sisters, but they do have a very strong tendency to achieve abilities in the same *order* as all other children. Certain abilities almost invariably precede or follow certain other abilities. This occurs because the development of the nervous system follows a predictable path. The nervous system grows *cephalocaudally:* that is, the baby's head and face control develops first, followed by development of the neck and trunk, the hands, and finally the legs and feet. You can see some evidence for this by looking at a nude newborn baby. Notice how much more developed and adultlike is his control of mouth and eyes than his control of his neck. Compare the physical development of his arms and hands to his almost nonexistent buttocks, his scrawny legs, and his fetal-appearing feet. The strength and control of the musculature in each case are an index of the development of the underlying nerves.

The Motor Milestones

The achievements which most clearly show the progress of cephalocaudal development are commonly called the *milestones of motor* development. Tables 6, 7, and 8 show a list of the milestones, which are easy to recognize as genuine advances in the baby's control of his body.

Table 6
The development of erect posture and locomotion

1   Tensing the muscles when lifted
2   Sitting with support
3   Lifting the head when lying on the back
4   Sitting alone momentarily
5   Standing with support under the armpits
6   Sitting alone
7   Standing with support by holding
8   Sitting down from the standing position
9   Pulling self to the standing position
10   Standing alone

(From *A Child's World: Infancy through Adolescence* by D. Papalia and S. Olds, p. 155. Copyright © 1975. Used with permission of McGraw-Hill Book Company.)

Table 7
Development of postural control and locomotion

Stage	Median Age, Weeks
First-order Skills. Passive Postural Control of Upper Trunk	
On stomach, chin up	3.0
On stomach, chest up	9.0
Held erect, stepping	13.0
On back, tense for lifting	15.0
Held erect, knees straight	15.0
Sit on lap, support at lower ribs and complete head control	18.5
Second-order Skills: Postural Control of Entire Trunk	
Sit alone momentarily	25.0
On stomach, knee push or swim	25.0
On back, rolling	29.0
Held erect, stand firmly with help	29.5
Sit alone, one minute	31.0
Third-order Skills: Active Attempts at Locomotion	
On stomach, some progress	37.0
On stomach, scoot backward	39.5
Fourth-order Skills: Locomotion and Improved Postural Control of Body	
Stand holding to furniture	42.0
Creep	44.5
Walk when led	45.0
Pull to stand by furniture	47.0

(From *A Child's World: Infancy through Adolescence* by D. Papalia and S. Olds, p. 155. Copyright © 1975. Used with permission of McGraw-Hill Book Company.)

Table 8
The course of motor development

Birth	Motor behavior is highly variable and transient. Wakefulness is not sharply differentiated from sleep. Infant does not stay in one position for any length of time. Exhibits reflex behaviors. Turns head from side to side while lying on back, lifts head for short time when prone, but head sags when not supported.

1 Month	Head still not self-supporting.
	Stares at surroundings.
	Some eye-following.
	Lifts chin when prone.
2 Months	Lifts chest.
	Holds head erect when held.
3 Months	Steps when held erect.
	Holds head erect and steady.
	Reaches for ball but misses.
	Turns from side to back.
4 Months	Head steady and self-supporting, lifts when prone, holds steady when held.
	Hands open and close.
	Reaches for objects close by but can't quite get them.
	Contemplates objects held in hand.
	Recognizes bottle.
	Eyes follow more distant objects.
	Plays with hands and clothing.
	Holds up chest.
	Shakes and stares at rattle placed in hand.
	Sits with support.
5 Months	Sits on lap.
	Grasps objects.
	Rolls over (not accidentally) from back to side.
6 Months	When sitting, bends forward and uses hands for support.
	Can bear weight when put in standing position, but cannot yet stand by holding on.
	Reaches with one hand.
	No thumb apposition yet in grasp. Can transfer objects from hand to hand.
	Releases cube held in hand when given another cube.
7 Months	Sits alone, without support, for a while.
	Holds head up.
	Attempts to crawl.
	Rolls over from back to stomach.
8 Months	Stands with help.
	Crawls (abdomen on floor, arms pull along body and legs).
	Shows thumb apposition.

24

10 Months	Creeps on hands and knees (trunk free; arms and legs alternate).
	Sits up easily.
	Pulls up to standing position.
	Can put one object on top of another.
12 Months	Walks with support.
	Seats self on floor.
13 Months	Climbs stair steps.
	Sits down.
14 Months	Stands alone.
15 Months	Walks alone.
18 Months	Runs in clumsy fashion, falls a lot.
	Can build tower of two or three objects.
	Pulls and pushes toys.
	Grasp, prehension, and reach are fully developed.
2 Years	Walks well.
	Runs fairly well, with a wide stance.
	Kicks large ball.
	Walks upstairs and downstairs alone.
	Builds tower of three objects.
	Jumps 12 inches.
	Turns pages of a book, one at a time.
2½ Years	Jumps into air with both feet.
	Stands on one foot about two seconds.
	Takes a few steps on tiptoe.
	Jumps from chair.
	Good hand-finger coordination.
	Can move fingers independently.
	Builds tower of five blocks.
3 Years	Stands on one foot.
	Rides tricycle.
	Draws circle.
	Pours from pitcher.
	Buttons and unbuttons.
	Tiptoes.
	Improved object manipulation.
	Can build six-cube tower.
	Runs smoothly.
	Walks up and down steps with alternate footing.

(From *A Child's World: Infancy through Adolescence* by D. Papalia and S. Olds, pp. 149–51. Copyright © 1975. Used by permission of the McGraw-Hill Book Company.)

Parents usually notice most of the milestones and make much of the baby for his progress. But the baby does not keep on with his sitting or his crawling for the reward of praise; he does it because the new activity is temporarily the most fascinating thing in the world. He does it for the sake of doing it, not because of the rewards or punishments it may bring him. This is very evident in the newly walking child, who may prance barefoot over sharp pebbles or prickly grass without appearing to notice. A few months later, when walking is taken for granted, he objects vociferously to discomfort underfoot. The brand-new walker may practice what one might call recreational walking. He walks just in order to walk; when he really wants to get somewhere, he crawls instead. You may even see the developing child carrying on a new activity in the absence of anything to do it to. For example, when he is de-

Figure 7.
The development of grasping. (From H. M. Halverson, "An Experimental Study of Prehension in Infants by Means of Systematic Cinema Records," *Genetic Psychology Monographs*, 1931, *10*, p. 212. Reprinted by permission of The Journal Press.)

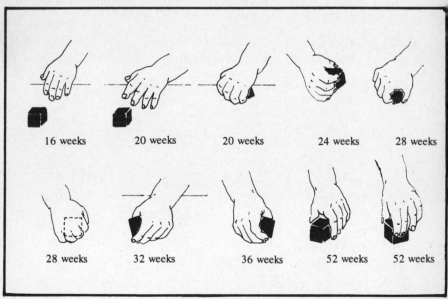

16 weeks	20 weeks	20 weeks	24 weeks	28 weeks
28 weeks	32 weeks	36 weeks	52 weeks	52 weeks

veloping the ability to grasp with his fingers (see Figure 7), he will go around "picking up nothing." He walks into the room, squats, and carefully grasps at the floor, then walks to his mother with fingers tightly pressed together. He proffers the gift to his mother, who holds out her hand for it—and he solemnly places in her hand nothing whatsoever. He did not fail to grasp the object; he did not drop it as he crossed the room; there was no object, but only a powerful need to practice picking up and releasing.

The sequence of the motor milestones has some implications for the child's comfort and safety. For instance, when a prone baby can lift his chest, you know that one of the next milestones to appear will be the ability to turn from side to back. Thus, he is no longer safe left lying unrestrained on a dressing table or a bed. When he can stand with help, he will soon be able to pull himself to a standing position and is not safe left in a crib with the side down. When he can sit with support, he will soon be able to grasp objects and is not safe left close to knives. Similarly, a baby who does not yet sit with support is not likely to be comfortable in the usual backpack carrier. A baby who still leans forward and supports himself with his hands when sitting will need a lap belt to make him comfortable in his high chair, or else will need the tray moved very close to him so he doesn't fall forward.

Although the cephalocaudal sequence does most to determine the order in which a baby's abilities develop, the chances he has to do certain things also make a difference. For instance, most charts of the milestones of motor development show babies crawling before they can pull themselves to a standing position. But ask most mothers today and they will tell you that their babies pulled to stand *before* they crawled. Why? It all seems to depend on what the baby has to pull on. If he has a modern mesh-sided playpen, it is very easy for him to hook his fingers in the mesh and pull up bit by bit. If he has the old-fashioned slat-sided kind, or if he is restricted to chair and table legs, he must wait until his grasp is a good deal stronger before he can pull himself up. Similarly, you may read about the Piagetian reach—a sequence in which the baby looks at an object, looks at his hand and moves it toward the object, looks back at the object, and so on, until the hand reaches the object. This sequence is much less frequently seen since the development of the tilted baby chair, which allows the infant to look around a great deal and see objects other than his hand.

One peculiarity of development seems to involve the amount of practice a baby puts in before he can successfully perform a new activity. Some babies can be observed making effort after effort to roll over or crawl, until they finally succeed. Others will show no apparent interest in the upcoming milestone, but will suddenly roll perfectly or crawl away or speak a clear word, without previous practice. This sudden achievement may be preceded by a few days of crankiness which clears up miraculously with the new achievement.

Variability is the rule about children's motor development. Although all children follow pretty much the same developmental pattern, there is tremendous variation in the exact ages at which different children arrive at particular stages. A child may begin to walk at any age between 10 and 19 months and still be well within the normal range. There is not necessarily a great advantage in exceptionally early development, nor is there a strong correlation between early motor development and later academic success.

Sphincter Control

The age at which a baby walks gives one important piece of information about him. It tells when he is *physically* ready for toilet training. If a baby walks, the nervous system must have developed to the point where it can control the movements of the lower part of the body. Thus it should be possible for the baby to learn voluntary control over the sphincter muscles of the bladder and bowels. As we will see in a later chapter, physical readiness for toilet training is not necessarily accompanied by emotional or intellectual readiness. However, you can be sure that a child who cannot yet walk is *not* ready to be toilet trained.

The Skipped Milestone

In recent years, a theory based on the sequence of motor milestones has caused worry to some parents and teachers. Delacato and others (Cratty, 1970) have put forward the idea that a brain-damaged child who has trouble controlling his body may benefit from "patterning"—a series of exercises which make the child go through the movements a baby shows in the course of cephalocaudal development. Whether "patterning" is effective with brain-damaged children is too complex a question to discuss here. The problem is that parents of normal children have somehow become concerned that their babies, in order to remain healthy, *must* show evidence of each of the motor milestones, as if they had to touch all bases in order to make a home run. In fact, many perfectly healthy children will skip a stage and go straight on to the next milestone. Most commonly, crawling is omitted, and the child goes directly from sitting to walking. Some parents have responded by trying to force the baby to crawl, fearing that if he does not he will be clumsy, have trouble learning to read, and so on. This situation is very frustrating for everyone in the family, and it creates a completely unnecessary problem where none exists. In fact, no child will do anything he is not ready to do. If he is not ready to walk, he won't be able to walk. When he is able, he is ready. And when he is ready, as we said earlier, walking becomes of paramount importance to him. Incredible frustration is generated when anyone tries to stop this totally fascinating activity. (However, if a child who had been sitting for a while could no longer do so, or a child who had been walking well reverted to crawling, there would indeed be cause for alarm.)

Inducing Early Walking

Babies apparently can be encouraged to walk unusually early by special exercises in the first few months of life. A considerable controversy has arisen from this fact.

The newborn baby, as we noted in Chapter 1, shows a *stepping reflex* when held in certain positions. This reflex normally disappears after a few months. But, if the parents exercise the reflex by holding the baby vertical and straightening its knees for some minutes each day, the stepping reflex will not disappear but will continue to be shown long after its normal time. Babies who are given this treatment seem to walk unusually early.

Some researchers (Pontius, 1973) now feel that babies who are induced to walk early may suffer impaired neuromuscular development. Normally, the dropping out of the newborn's reflexes indicates that the cortex is developing and suppressing the reflexes so that voluntary movement may result instead. If the reflexes are maintained, this might mean that the normal relationship between the cortex and the lower brain centers has been disrupted. Until there is more definite evidence about the long-range effects of maintaining the stepping reflex, it would probably be better for parents not to try to induce early walking in this way. A few months one way or the other in the child's development of walking will not make a great deal of difference in convenience for the parents. And, if the desire to have the child walk early is based on competition with other families, parents might ask themselves whether winning this kind of race is worth even a slight risk of harm to the child.

Growth

The first year of life is a period of rapid growth and change. The rate of growth of the fetus slows down just before birth, but immediately after birth there is a period of catching up when the rate of weight gain is very high. Then the rate gradually slows as the child progresses toward his first birthday, as Figure 8 shows. Even when the rate has slowed, of course, the baby is still gaining very quickly relative to his body size. At the rate shown for fifty weeks of age in Figure 8, the baby would gain eight pounds per year. Since he probably weighs only twenty-two pounds or so at this age, he is adding weight at the rate of about thirty-five percent a year. For a hundred-fifty-pound adult to do this would mean gaining fifty pounds in a year. It's no wonder babies are so impatient for their meals. Breast-fed babies may respond to periods of rapid growth by demanding constant nursing. The effect of frequent suckling is to build up the mother's milk production and provide sufficient calories to support the infant's spurt in growth. As for the use of solid food in the early months, the feeding of solids before three months of age does not increase the nutritional adequacy of the diet, or the calorie intake. The infant absorbs almost no iron from solid food at this age. One researcher has "questioned the wisdom of such a procedure before the child is three months old, since the infant has no need for the additional nutrients, is not physiologically and developmentally capable of handling them, and may experience an increased susceptibility to allergy" (Guthrie, 1966, p. 879).

The relationship between growth and appetite works the

Figure 8.
Growth rate of single-born children. (From J. M. Tanner, "The Regulation of Human Growth," *Child Development*, 1963, *34*, pp. 817-48. Reprinted by permission of The Society for Research in Child Development, Inc.)

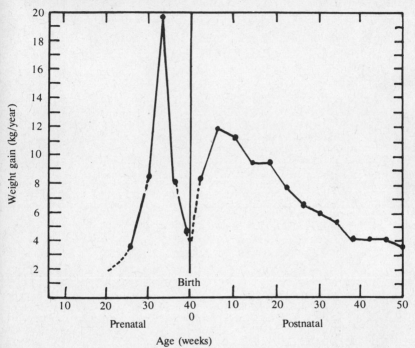

other way around, too, and it is not surprising that as the baby's rate of growth slows he eats less and less. This loss of appetite is not necessarily a sign of illness or "feeding problems," but indicates that the child actually needs less than he did before. (The loss of appetite can produce some nutritional problems in the slightly older child, since he can sometimes satisfy his caloric needs completely by drinking milk, but does not get all the vitamins he needs in that way.)

When we talk about a baby's growth rate, it sounds as if every bit of him is growing at exactly the same rate. This is most

Figure 9.

Rates of growth of different parts and tissues of the body. (From L. Carmichael (ed.), *Manual of Child Psychology*, New York: John Wiley and
Sons, Inc., 1946, p. 364. Used by permission.)

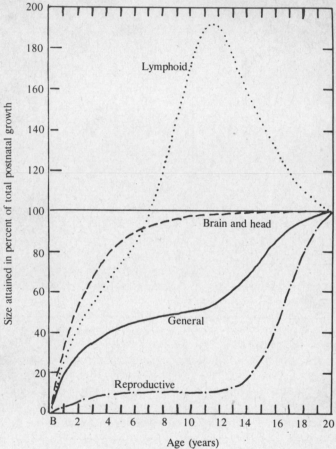

definitely not the case. Figure 9 shows the rates of growth of different parts of children's bodies at different ages. You can see how
slowly the reproductive tissues grow early in life, and the very
rapid growth of the brain and head.

Since different parts of the child are growing at different
rates, his shape is bound to change between the newborn period

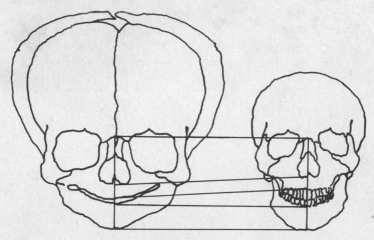

Figure 10.

Changes in facial proportions with growth. The skull on the left is that of a newborn baby; on the right is an adult's skull. The distance from the bottom of the chin to the lower lip has been drawn equal so that the differences in proportion can be seen. (From *Developmental Psychology Today,* p. 108. Copyright © 1971 CRM Books, a division of Random House, Inc. Adapted from the original in *Morris Human Anatomy,* C. M. Jackson (ed.), P. Blakiston's Sons and Co., 1923. Used with permission of McGraw-Hill Book Company.)

and later ages. Part of the change in shape is dictated by the rule of cephalocaudal development; as growth proceeds, the newborn baby's big head and tiny buttocks give way to the leggy look of the five-year-old. But even within a single part of the body, changes in proportions can be seen. Figure 10 shows how the proportions of the face change between birth and adulthood. The newborn baby, whose skull is shown on the left, has a big forehead, big eyes, and a small jaw and chin, in comparison to the proportions of the adult skull on the right. (Incidentally, the baby's proportions have the characteristics of "cuteness," as seen in puppies, kittens, and Walt Disney cartoon animals. Small mouth, small chin, large ears, and large forehead produce a feeling of attraction in adults.)

The lengthening of the baby's legs and arms makes him act as well as look more adult. The increase in height makes it possible for him to reach things on top of tables, to climb out of his crib, and to walk holding an adult's hand without great discomfort to both. Although the baby's length at birth does not predict very well how tall he will be as an adult, his height as a toddler does. A girl's adult height is likely to be about twice her height at her second birthday, whereas a boy is likely to grow to about twice the height he has reached at two and a half.

One important aspect of early growth involves the development of bones. Months before birth, the fetus' skeleton consists entirely of cartilage. Gradually minerals are deposited in the cartilage and it turns to bone. But this process is by no means complete at birth. In Figure 11, we can see the difference in bone structure of the hands of a six-month-old and a five-year-old. Many of the six-month-old's bones are still soft and incomplete. Because of the softness of the bones, deformities like clubfoot can be corrected by casts or special shoes at an early age. (Deformities can also be *produced* by ill-fitting shoes.) The soft bones of young children are more likely to be bent or partly splintered (greenstick fracture) by a fall than snapped like those of adults. The incompleteness of the bones gives the young child's hand a squishy feeling, which sometimes makes adults feel the hand will come off if they pull too hard on a reluctant youngster. The incompleteness of the baby's skull, as seen in the fontanel, is just one example of skeletal immaturity.

Growth is largely dependent on an innate biological pattern and on nutrition. It can also be affected by psychological stress and by certain drugs.

A child under profound emotional stress may develop the syndrome of deprivation dwarfism. Such a child simply stops growing at an early age. He may appear relatively healthy and may eat and drink enormous amounts, but he still fails to grow. Sometimes a similar state is a result of malfunctioning of the pituitary gland. In the case of deprivation dwarfism, however, the cause of failure to grow is an emotional one. The state may begin when a child loses parental attention because of the birth of a new baby, or when illness or death of the parents causes loss of the experience of love. On the other hand, if the child's parents simply do not care about him, his failure to grow may be reversed if he is placed in a foster home where he gets plenty of attention.

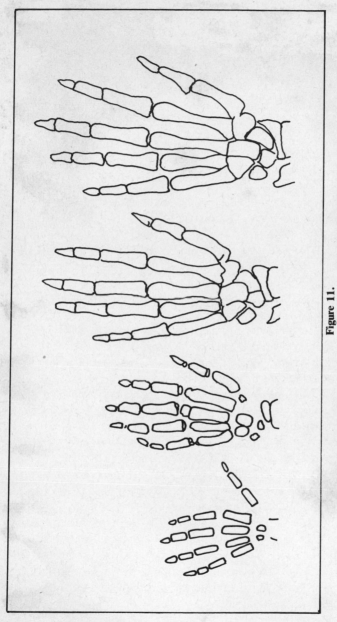

Figure 11.

Changes in skeletal structure between birth and maturity.

35

Some drugs used in treatment of the behavior disorder hyperkinesis can also stunt growth. Certain stimulants used to treat the hyperkinetic child prevent normal growth both in height and in weight.

Sex Differences

Boys and girls *are* different. This fact complicates any description of the way children grow and change in the first year of life. In early childhood as well as in adulthood, there are genuine sex differences which are the result of biology and not of culture.

Three general differences exist between young male and female children. First, being male is a *biological disadvantage*. More male than female fetuses are miscarried, and more male than female babies die in the first month of life.

Second, males are more *variable* than females. Although the average intelligence quotient of males is about the same as that of females, there are more very bright males than females and more severely retarded males than females.

Third, in early life females seem to have a *developmental advantage* as measured by skeletal age—the extent to which the cartilage skeleton has been transformed into bone. At birth boys are about four weeks behind girls in skeletal maturity. Right up until sexual maturity boys have a skeletal age which is only about eighty percent of that shown by girls of the same chronological age. Girls are also advanced over boys in dental age, or the maturity of the tooth pattern. "Girls are usually ahead of boys in motor development also and in certain forms of aptitude tests" (Tanner, 1970, p. 109). Perhaps this early developmental superiority of the female has to do with the earlier sexual maturity of girls; they have a more hurried timetable on which they proceed to puberty, whereas boys have more time to complete skeletal growth, and so on, before puberty overtakes them.

The rates of growth shown in early life are different for boys and for girls. The average newborn boy is growing slightly faster than the average newborn girl, but by about seven months their growth rates are about equal. Then girls grow a little faster up to about four years. Between four and the beginning of puberty, the growth rates are about equal.

The growth rate and development of girls are less influenced by stress than those of boys. Malnutrition slows the rate of a child's growth, but it does so more for males than for females. Even in the case of genetic damage to brain function like trisomy-21 (mongolism), girls with this problem show higher intelligence quotients than boys with the same sort of damage.

Sex differences in basal metabolic rate (rate of burning of food and oxygen by the body) exist from the age of 1 month on, with boys showing a higher metabolic rate relative to their height than girls (although there is no difference in infancy if the BMR is calculated relative to weight).

Obviously, sex differences amount to more than the possession of a penis or a vagina. They govern a number of aspects of early development. But, of course, these biological sex differences are reinforced by cultural factors which cause boys and girls to be treated differently from infancy. These factors will be dealt with in a later chapter.

Social Development: Crying

In the previous chapter we discussed the reasons why newborn babies cry. One of the profound changes of the first year of life is the change from a strictly biological organism to a social one—and, as a result, the beginning of crying for social reasons.

Even by the end of the second week of life, a human voice becomes more effective than other noises in stopping a baby's crying. In another week, a new development has occurred: whether something makes the baby cry or stops it depends on the state of comfort of the baby. A baby of three weeks may smile if he hears a voice or certain other sounds, *provided* that he is already alert but quiet. If he is unhappy or fussing or wriggling, the same sounds may touch off full-fledged crying. "The clearest indication of this relation between state and affective response is the fussy baby's response to a silent, nodding head. Although the silent face as yet elicits no smiling in the third week, it precipitates an immediate cry face or even full-fledged cry vocalizations when presented to the fussy baby, whether it is the face of the mother, a familiar observer, or a stranger. As soon as the face disappears, the baby stops crying; and by repeating this sequence until the baby gets desperate, one can demonstrate that it is a visual stimulus rather than an unknown factor which provokes the cry under the conditions described" (Wolff, 1970). In other words, grandmas or kind strangers need not feel offended when the young baby cries upon seeing them—any face would have the same effect if the baby was already fussy. But by eight months or so, there is a definite fear of strangers (see Chapter 3).

Social Development: Smiling

The infant may begin his social life by crying in response to other people, but a social smile is also one of his abilities after he reaches about six weeks of age. (Before that time, reflexive smiling may occur as a result of gas bubbles or when the lips are touched.) When social smiling begins, it occurs in response to faces. In the beginning, any face will do, but as time passes, familiar and/or smiling faces receive more smiles from the baby. The continuing development of the social smile depends on the responses of adults to the baby's smiles. Babies living in families show an increasing rate of smiling during the first months of their lives, but babies in orphanages do not.

Perceiving the World

The newborn baby very probably does not see the world as his parents do. For one thing, when the objects he sees have no meaning because he has had no experience with them, they are bound to seem less interesting and important than the state of his skin or bowels. For adults, the visual world is the most interesting and informative aspect of perception.

For the newborn infant, as we mentioned earlier, the distance at which vision is clearest is about eight inches from an object. This means that most objects in his world will appear fuzzy and blurry. With increasing age, the baby develops the capacity of *accommodation:* changing the focus of the eyes so that both near and distant objects can be seen clearly. By the time he reaches three months of age, he can change focus about as well as an adult can.

The baby must also develop *visual constancy.* This is a long process which probably occurs as a result of experience rather than of biological maturation. Constancy is the capacity to recognize objects as the same things even when the pictures we get of them are different because of changes in angle, distance, lighting, and so on. Try looking at a distant person with the naked eye and then through a rolled-up paper or the cardboard tube from a roll of paper towels. You will see that the person looks smaller when you use the tube so that you see only him and none of the objects around him. Constancy allows you to compare the size of a person to the size of other objects and to recognize that he is still the same size as usual, even though his image on your eye has become smaller with distance. Now, the baby, who has not yet developed visual constancy, probably cannot compare the size of various images and come to accurate conclusions about the world. Instead, as his mother gets farther away and her image becomes smaller, the baby may think she is shrinking, or even that he is seeing a succession of smaller and smaller women, each different from the others. No wonder it takes a while before babies can tell their parents apart from other adults. They must first learn to recognize that mother-at-the-door is the same individual as mother-bending-over-the-crib—not to speak of learning that mother is the same person with or without her glasses, frowning or smiling, with hair straight or curly, and whether wearing a red dress or blue jeans.

Babies seem to be born with *or* to develop very early the capacity for *depth perception*. This can be demonstrated with an apparatus called a visual cliff. A transparent Plexiglas top is suspended so that part of it is just over a table and another part has no apparent support between it and the floor. Crawling babies (and, indeed, the young of most or all mammals) will not crawl out onto the "deep side," where it looks as if they will fall through, but are willing to crawl onto the "shallow side." They want not only to be supported (by the Plexiglas) but also to appear to be supported (by the underlying table). Even babies too young to crawl show a change in heart rate depending on whether they are held over the deep or the shallow side of the visual cliff.

People who are experienced with babies may reply to the evidence of the visual cliff, "if babies are so good at depth perception, why are they always falling off things?" This tendency to fall off anything they can find has been referred to as the "Geronimo response." It may occur simply because the baby has no idea how far he can lean over before he loses his balance. Or, he may be concentrating so hard on a physical activity like pulling himself to a standing position that he is not able to look around him at the same time.

Language

A crucial difference between the newborn and the one-year-old is the capacity to understand some spoken words (and, for some 1-year-olds, to speak some). Like some visual abilities, this skill develops as the result of experience. The child must hear speech in order to learn to understand it, and he must hear it under good circumstances. For instance, the ghetto baby, living in over-crowded conditions, may hear words addressed to him only against a background of television and noisy conversation, while a more privileged infant hears voices talking to him while everything else is quiet. The first child may find it hard to separate words from all the other noises he is hearing, just as adults find it hard to concentrate on a single conversation at a loud party. He is, in fact, in the process of suffering from genuine cultural depriva-tion (not just exposure to a different culture), because he is not getting to experience language, the principal expression of human culture.

Under good circumstances, babies show signs of under-standing some words as early as six or seven months of age. Under-standing comes much earlier than speaking. It is shown by looking toward the door when someone says "Daddy's coming" or other actions which show that a word has meaning, that it signals an event which has not yet begun.

Chapter 3
Children Have Temperaments

There is reason to believe that biological factors create certain temperamental qualities which are present in the child at birth and which stay with him throughout his life. Some of these factors may affect the way the parents respond to the baby and thus help determine how he learns to behave. Experience with brothers and sisters and the effects of birth order also help to create lifelong behavior patterns.

For fifty or sixty years, American parents have read and heard that a child's behavior depends entirely on his upbringing. The popularity of behaviorism led to the idea that, whether a child behaves well or badly, the cause of his behavior can be traced to the ways his parents treat him. Many people have felt that (if they only knew how) they could have complete control over the way their children acted. This idea dates back to the famous statement of John B. Watson, the founder of American behaviorism, who declared that, given a dozen healthy children and the right environments, he could produce at will "doctor, lawyer, merchant chief" or any other desired adult.

Obviously, what a child learns does have a great deal to do

with his later behavior. No one today would claim that any of the complexities of human behavior were brought about solely by heredity. But, as the years passed after Watson's emphatic statement, it became apparent that the behavior of subhuman animals is often genetically determined. And, in many cases, no amount of reward or punishment will eradicate the hereditary behavior. Students of child development began to wonder whether humans, too, might have some behaviors which were determined by their genetic backgrounds. They also began to ask whether all babies were indeed alike at the time of birth.

Now, any parent of many children or any obstetric nurse knows that all newborn babies are different in their basic ways of reacting to the world. Babies differ in *temperament*, in their tendencies to respond to stimulation in one way or another. The questions to be answered by research are two. First, how many different temperaments are there? In how many ways can newborn babies differ from each other? Second, is the temperament something which is consistent throughout life? If you know how a baby acts at six months of age, can you predict how he will act at one year, or five years, or in adulthood?

Temperamental Qualities

One group of researchers (Chess, Thomas, and Birch, 1965) has found nine temperamental characteristics which appear to remain more or less consistent from two months of age until at least ten years of age. Here, in brief, are the nine temperamental qualities:

1. *Activity level:* a child may be quiet or active, slow or quick in his movements, able or unable to sit still.
2. *Rhythmicity:* a child may have regular or irregular patterns of sleeping, waking, eating, and eliminating.
3. *Distractibility:* a child may continue to concentrate in spite of distractions, or he may stop whatever he is doing whenever anything novel occurs.
4. *Approach/withdrawal:* a child may cheerfully try anything new, or he may be negative and suspicious about unfamiliar things.
5. *Adaptability:* a child may quickly get used to something new, even though he disliked it at first, or he may continue to object after many exposures to the new situation.

6. *Attention span and persistence:* a child may continue to try to accomplish what he wants in spite of a long period of frustration, or he may give up easily.

7. *Intensity of reaction:* a child may be vigorous in acceptance or rejection of a situation, or he may be relatively bland and unenthusiastic.

8. *Threshold of responsiveness:* a baby may require very little stimulation (noise, tickling, and so on) to make him respond, or he may ignore all but strong stimulation.

9. *Quality of mood:* a child may be generally cheerful and positive, even in the absence of specific stimulation, or generally fussy and negative.

The criteria used by Thomas, Chess, and Birch to rate a child on each of the nine temperamental qualities are shown in Table 9. Of course, the behavior we look at to decide whether a two-

Table 9
Characteristics of "Difficult" and "Easy" Babies

| | TYPE OF CHILD | | |
	"EASY"	"SLOW TO WARM UP"	"DIFFICULT"
ACTIVITY LEVEL	Varies	Low to moderate	Varies
RHYTHMICITY	Very regular	Varies	Irregular
DISTRACTIBILITY	Varies	Varies	Varies
APPROACH/WITHDRAWAL	Positive approach	Initial withdrawal	Withdrawal
ADAPTABILITY	Very adaptable	Slowly adaptable	Slowly adaptable
ATTENTION SPAN	High or low	High or low	High or low
INTENSITY OF REACTION	Low or mild	Mild	Intense
THRESHOLD OF RESPONSIVENESS	High or low	High or low	High or low
MOOD QUALITY	Positive	Slightly negative	Negative

(From A. Thomas, S. Chess, and H. G. Birch, "The Origin of Personality." Copyright © 1970 by *Scientific American, Inc.,* August, pp. 106-107. All rights reserved.)

month-old is highly active is different from that to be observed in the two-year-old, five-year-old, or ten-year-old, so a series of criteria appropriate for different age levels is needed.

Thomas, Chess, and Birch have grouped certain temperamental qualities together in order to judge a baby as "easy," "difficult," or "slow to warm up." Table 9 shows the categories which help define a baby's "easiness." About sixty-five percent of the children in this study could be categorized while the other thirty-five percent showed a mixture of traits.

A large proportion of the "difficult" children in this study later developed behavior problems, while only a small number of the "easy" children did so. But this should not be taken to mean that the parents of these children had nothing to do with their behavior. "Difficult" babies do not automatically develop into problem children, nor do "easy" babies necessarily remain easy. Certain child-rearing techniques will encourage a difficult baby to become easier to get along with, while others may make an easy baby hard to cope with.

According to Thomas, Chess, and Birch, easy children are generally no problem to raise, no matter what style the parents use. In certain cases, the easy child may conform to the parents' expectations in early life, but may have trouble learning that life with his peers and at school requires him to adapt to a different set of requirements. It may be hard for the child to deal with such a double standard after a long experience of complete success in conforming to the parents' wishes. Thomas, Chess, and Birch have described the case of a little girl called Isobel whose parents had encouraged her to be imaginative and expressive. On entering school, Isobel learned poorly and made few friends. She had learned to value her individuality so highly that it was difficult for her to be told what to do by her teacher or to play the way the other children wanted her to. When her parents worked with her on cooperation with other people, she soon improved in all areas of school life.

Difficult children, on the other hand, present many problems from the beginning because of their irregularity and slowness of conformity to the family's rules. Impatience or punishment provoke unusually negative reactions. These children can learn to cooperate and function well, but they must be handled especially carefully.

Children who are "slow to warm up," according to Thomas, Chess, and Birch, must be allowed to develop at their own rate, but they should be encouraged to try new things. Pressure to try something new makes this sort of child tend to withdraw, but if he is simply let alone he will not try anything unfamiliar. Parents and teachers should try to establish a balance which makes new experiences available but does not force any issues.

Thomas, Chess, and Birch have suggested that a child's temperament may fit well or poorly with different school situations. The "slow to warm up" child may need to be exposed to a learning task many times before he is ready to deal with it, no matter what his basic intelligence level may be. In this era of open classrooms, it is interesting to note Thomas, Chess, and Birch's suggestions that difficult or easily distracted children may need constant firm supervision from their teacher.

In looking over the temperamental quality scales for different ages, we see that a quality may be desirable or undesirable, depending on the age of the child. Take the quality of distractibility, for instance. The baby of six months who is not distractible can be a real nuisance. He cries while being dressed, no matter how his mother sings and makes faces at him. He cries until his bottle is ready and is not temporarily satisfied by seeing his mother preparing his meal. The same child at ten years of age has some real advantages: he can read without being distracted even if someone else has a loud television show on, and he remembers to do his chores when he is supposed to. The distractible six-month-old stops crying in response to a song or a toy, but the same child at ten cannot do his homework unless the household is completely quiet. So, although a child may never "grow out of" a particular quality of temperament, he may grow into a stage where the expression of the quality is much more acceptable to adults.

Some other researchers have looked at specific behavior of the newborn which seems related to particular behavior when the child reaches nursery-school age. In some cases, one kind of behavior in the newborn leads to a particular behavior at preschool age for both boys and girls. In other cases, the newborn's behavior is predictive of later activity only for one sex. For instance, new-born boys who cried a lot when a nipple was taken away from them tended as preschoolers to watch other children play and be inactive in games. For girls, there was no relation between response to the loss of the nipple and their later play involvement. On the other hand, newborn babies who were unusually sensitive to touch later showed poor concentration on achievement of a goal, whether they were boys or girls. Thus, the whole matter of predicting later behavior from the way the newborn acts may be complicated by sex differences. (For a more complete presentation of the relation between newborn and later behavior, see Tables 10 and 11.)

The interaction between a baby and his mother is determined to some extent by his responsiveness from the time of birth onward. A mother is more likely to be attentive and affectionate to a

Table 10
Behaviors showing clear relations between newborn and later periods in both sexes

Newborn period	*Preschool period*	
	Males	*Females*
Low sensitivity to touch	Vigorous attack on barriers; sustained goal orientation	Same as males, plus liveliness, good coordination
High sensitivity to touch	Lethargic and briefly sustained goal orientation	Same as males; also inactivity and clumsiness
Rapid respiration at highest point in sleep	Inattentive to sounds, inactive in producing sounds	Inattentive to music or books
Slow respiration at highest point in sleep	Attentive to sounds, active in producing sounds	Attentive to music and books
Slow respiration at lowest point in sleep	Advanced speech, communication, and imitation of adults	Same as males

(Adapted from R. Q. Bell, G. M. Weller, and M. F. Waldrop, "Newborn and Preschooler: Organization of Behavior and Relations Between Periods," *Monographs of the Society for Research in Child Development*, 1971, *36*, p. 115. Reprinted by permission of The Society for Research in Child Development, Inc.)

Table 11
**Behaviors showing most clear relations between newborn
and later periods in one sex only**

Newborn period	Preschool period	
	Males	Females
Rapid respiration at highest or lowest points in sleep	Lethargic and passive in free play; unfriendly	No relation shown
Slow response, few cries after nipple removal	Active and interested in games and rituals	No relation shown
High, sustained head lifting when prone	No relation shown	Restlessness; high motor activity; negative emotions; easily awakened
Many mouth movements during sleep	No relation shown	Advanced speech(?)
Large feedings relative to birth weight	No relation shown	Active, assertive, gregarious
Small feedings relative to birth weight	No relation shown	Lethargic, passive in free play; unfriendly

(Adapted from R. Q. Bell, G. M. Weller, and M. J. Waldrop, "Newborn and Preschooler: Organization of Behavior and Relations Between Periods," *Monographs of the Society for Research in Child Development,* 1971, 36 p. 116. Reprinted by permission of The Society for Research in Child Development, Inc.)

baby who responds to her than she is to one who is passive or who reacts primarily to his internal sensations. The baby's responsiveness seems to be related to other characteristics shown during the neonatal period (Osofsky and Danzgar, 1974). Babies who make good eye contact with the mother and respond well to her voice are also alert and easily consoled when upset. They are able to get their hands in their mouths at an early age, and they protest strongly over painful stimulation. These general signs of good development at birth go with a good experience in the baby's first social relationship—that with his mother. The baby who is born less well developed is likely to get off to a poorer social start.

Occasionally one reads or hears of the idea that the brain functions of the newborn (as measured by the electroencephalograph) can be used to predict later intelligence or achievement. There does not seem to be any research evidence for a correlation between newborn EEG patterns and school achievement.

So far in this chapter we have been talking about the biological aspects of personality. But we can also consider here the effects of some general experiences on the development of personality. Some crucial aspects of the child's life may involve a general climate of experience rather than specific ways in which his parents treat him, and these may have an effect on his basic personality as strong as that of his biological make-up. Two such general experiences are *birth order* and *family constellation*.

Birth Order

The study of birth order and its relation to personality simply examines how whether a child is first or last born to his parents or in between affects personality development. The idea of the importance of birth order was first suggested by Alfred Adler, but has since been tested by a number of research studies. Here, in brief, are some of the conclusions of research on birth order (Toman, 1969).

1. Firstborns appear to have a greater need for achievement.
2. More firstborns go to college.
3. Firstborns marry earlier than later-borns.
4. Firstborns are less anxious about being tested than later-borns.
5. Firstborns choose less popular people as their friends than later-borns.
6. Firstborns are more often chosen than later-borns, when children are asked who their friends are.

Family Constellation

The general way in which a child is treated, the atmosphere in which he spends his formative years, is produced not only by his own position in the family, but also by the positions his parents occupied in their own families of birth. The relative positions of the father and mother and of all their children are termed the *family constellation*. It has been suggested (and some research supports this idea) that family constellation does much to determine social relationships, especially a person's long-lasting friendships or marriage.

The concept of family constellation goes beyond birth order theories in that it takes into account the sexes of siblings as well as their relative ages. Family constellation theory assumes that early relationships with older or younger people of the same or of the opposite sex determine how an adult will get along with different kinds of people. For instance, a girl with older brothers would be expected to have different kinds of social relationships in adulthood than a girl with younger brothers.

Obviously, this is a complex matter, for often a family will have a constellation which involves more than one kind of relationship. A girl may have one younger brother and one younger sister, or one older brother and one younger brother—or any of a multitude of other situations. In addition, the person's choices may be affected because of habits learned from a mother or father who had developed those habits because of a specific family constellation in the previous generation. These latter effects may be very important in determining how well parents get along with certain ones of their children.

A basic idea in the theory of family constellation is that people learn early about the relative rank, or seniority, or power, or other people, and that they use this information in forming their later social relationships. Ordinarily, the older child is more powerful and the younger ones weaker. Older children thus learn to take positions of power relative to other people, and younger children get used to having others make the decisions.

Similarly, people learn through early experience to be comfortable with people of the same or of the opposite sex. A girl who has sisters only is denied an important chance to get used to males, while a girl who has brothers only may not learn to be comfortable with her own sex. A child who has both male and female siblings gets used to the problems and advantages involved in living with both sexes and so has improved chances for success in marriage and in friendship.

Family constellation theory especially stresses the interaction of rank and of sex. The girl who has an older brother will be used to deferring to males, while the girl with a younger brother will be used to dominating and caring for them. The boy with a younger sister will grow up with the idea that females are weaker and more dependent, while the boy with an older sister will feel that females are strong and can be depended on. Thus a marriage between the brother of a younger sister and a girl who has an older brother is likely to provide a good meshing of attitudes. The husband is used to dominating, while the wife is used to being dominated. Each expects the other to act just as the other would naturally choose to act. But, when a brother of a younger sister marries the sister of a younger brother, conflicts are likely to occur. Both people are accustomed to dominating people of the opposite sex with whom they have close relationships—and, obviously, both cannot simultaneously be dominant.

Family constellation apparently makes a good deal of difference to friendships, both in childhood and in adulthood, and to the success of marriage. Parents should note, too, that it is important in the relationships between their children and themselves. The patterns of the parent's family constellation are reflected in the way he or she gets along with his/her own children.

The father who had no sisters does not really know, at least at the beginning, how to get along with girls. His relationship with his daughters is not likely to be as good as that with his sons. The reverse will be true if the father had sisters and no brothers. Mothers who have only brothers or only sisters have the same problem.

The parent's position in the birth order of his family plays an important part, too. Generally the parent gets along best with the child whose sibling position is complementary to the parent's; that is, the parent who was the oldest in his family deals best with the youngest of his children, while the parent who was the "baby" of his family deals best with the eldest of his offspring. But this situation is complicated by the sex of the siblings of parent and of child. The father who is the oldest brother of brothers may get along very well with his son who is the youngest brother of brothers, but the relationship might be far worse with a son who is the youngest brother of sisters, since in the latter case the father might resent the son's good relationship with girls, might want him to "be a man" and spend his time with other boys.

What happens to the only child? He may be in for considerable conflict if his parent of the same sex was also an only child, for "both of them would want to be the only one for the third member of the family" (Toman, p. 165). If both parents had brothers and sisters, though, the only child may learn from his same-sex parent to act like someone of the parent's sibling position.

The Effects of Family Constellation

A great deal of research has been done on the general consequences of being born into one family constellation or another. We will briefly present here a list of the conclusions of some of the more interesting studies (Toman, 1969). (Well-matched parents are ones whose positions as siblings are complementary; for example, a younger brother of sisters and a younger sister of brothers. Heterosexual constellations are those where a boy has only sisters or a girl only brothers; bisexual constellations are those where a boy or a girl has both brothers and sisters.)

1. More older sisters of brothers have well-adjusted sons, while more youngest sisters have problem children.
2. Leaders of youth groups are more likely to be oldest brothers or only children.
3. Physical aggression in school is more common among boys who have brothers only than in those from bisexual or heterosexual sibling groups.
4. Achievement motivation is higher in oldest and only children.

Chapter 4
The Developing Personality

Attachment to the parents and fear of strangers are a normal development of the first year of life; loss of the parents can be emotionally damaging at this time. Breast-feeding may or may not be very desirable from an emotional point of view, depending upon other family factors. Thumb-sucking is a common behavior in early life and does not necessarily indicate insecurity. Illness and surgery produce different reactions as the child matures, but hospitalization may have more serious effects than is usually thought. With maturity, defense mechanisms develop, so it is less easy to communicate with the child on emotional topics. Symptoms of emotional disturbance in childhood include social withdrawal, lack of impulse control, fire-setting, and cruelty to animals.

The term "personality" refers to all those characteristics which make a person unique—his hopes, fears, and habits, his attitudes, his motivations, his deepest needs. Some aspects of personality seem to be learned through experience in the course of childhood. Others are probably related to innate, biologically determined temperamental qualities (discussed in Chapter 3).

Both learned and innate personality characteristics are interesting from the developmental point of view. When we consider learning from experience, we must ask whether certain times in a child's life are critical periods when certain experiences will be extremely influential, while at other ages the child will be little affected by the same experiences. In thinking about innate aspects of personality, we can inquire whether particular tendencies are expressed according to a biological timetable, with little influence from parents' attempts at intervention. This chapter will deal with both aspects of personality growth.

Attachment and Separation Anxiety

The process of emotional attachment between mother and child begins early in life. At birth, of course, the baby does not seem to know the difference between his biological mother and any other person who cares for him. In the course of 5 or 6 months, however, he begins to discriminate between mother and stranger. By 8 months of age (on the average) he shows this discrimination by showing great anxiety and distress when separated from his mother or when approached by a stranger.

This fearful reaction to strangers at the end of the first year is embarrassing to parents, who want their child to be friendly and outgoing. Here is the baby, cheerful and happy—and when some innocent, friendly stranger comes along there are tears and howls of protest. If the parents want to leave the child with a new babysitter, considerable drama marks their departure. The age of separation anxiety is also an age of frantic expressions of dependency on the parents. An expressive, highly dependent child may begin to scream when his mother simply walks across the room. Babies who are unusually irritable about other things also express unusual distress about separation.

Separation anxiety is an expression of emotion, but it does not occur until the child is intellectually ready for it. The two-month-old baby does not cry when his mother leaves because he forgets her existence as soon as she is out of sight. He does not try to turn to look after her or start to fret when it is time for her to come home. He has not yet developed the concept of *object permanence,* the understanding that objects still exist when one cannot see them (see Chapter 2). After more months of development, however, he has begun to have some faith in the continued existence of the world. He is fairly sure his mother still exists—somewhere in the universe—and he wants her back.

The role of learning in separation anxiety is also shown in the fact that one-year-olds are more likely to be upset when left alone with a stranger if they come from families where there is little interaction with the father (Spelke et al., 1973). Infants also tend to respond more positively to strange children than to strange adults, and baby boys respond better to female than to male strangers (Greenberg, Hillman, and Grice, 1973).

On the surface, the baby's attachment and dependency seem to prevent him from exploring the world. In practice, though, he uses the parent as a base from which he ranges out and exercises his curiosity. A baby left alone or with a stranger in a room full of interesting toys may not get up the nerve to explore at all. When he is with his mother, on the other hand, he clings for a while, gets down and explores, comes back to cling again, then ranges even farther than before in his exploration. The satisfaction of his dependency needs allows him to refuel emotionally and to gain the confidence needed for confronting the world.

The period of separation anxiety is also a period when loss of the parents can have shattering effects. The baby is rightly anxious about separation, for actual loss of a parent at this age can have serious consequences. The bereaved baby grieves over its loss as no adult can ever do. Serious depression is one of the possible results of loss at this critical period. The baby loses interest in food, withdraws socially, and fails to grow or develop at its normal rate. Attention given by anyone other than the lost parent seems worthless, at least at the beginning; after a long time a patient foster parent may finally win the child's attachment.

The effect of loss is most serious when the lost person is the only one to whom a baby has been attached. When a number of people have cared for the baby, the attachment to any one is relatively diluted, and the effect of loss of any single individual is relatively small.

Some losses are sudden and unavoidable. Death and serious illness do not allow us to plan ahead to diminish the effect on a baby. But there are cases in which the effects of loss and separation can be minimized by careful handling. One historical example of such a situation was the evacuation of children from London during World War II. A similar set of circumstances for the child is seen when a marriage breaks up and one spouse leaves the household. Unfortunately, many people believe that a child in one of these situations "adjusts" more quickly if the change is made abruptly and if some weeks are allowed to pass before the separated parent comes to visit. Such an abrupt transition is indeed easier on the adult, who is spared the sight of the child's grief, but it is *not* easier on the child. If the child has a chance to see the departing parent every day for a few days, then every other day, and so on, there will be tears and distress at every parting, but the child will gradually work out his feelings with relatively few behavior problems. When the break is abrupt, the child is overwhelmed with distress too great to express through tears or words. By the time the parent comes to visit, the child does not cry or show much interest. He seems to have "forgotten"—but at the cost of turning all his energies toward coping with his despair. As a result, he is likely to regress in his behavior, to wet the bed, to use baby talk, to lose his capacity to share or take turns. Anna Freud has described a little boy named Patrick, evacuated from London during the war, who talked to himself constantly about how his mother would come to get him and would dress him and take him home. When he was reprimanded for this, he stopped talking about it, but developed a stereotyped ritual which represented zipping his coat, putting on his boots, and so on.

Attachment, Touching, and Swaddling

How does attachment develop? One might think it was a result of being fed by the mother and of her other efforts at physical care. But research on monkeys suggests that soft, warm skin contact is most important in establishing attachment.

Babies need to be touched, rocked, and cuddled, and they need these things in a physiological sense as well as a psychological sense. Mother cats and dogs, cows and sheep, lick their babies as they nurse; the babies actually need this physical contact in order to digest their food properly. Human babies in orphanages may gain little weight and show badly retarded development.

If they get the chance to be rocked, stroked, and cuddled, they begin to gain weight on the same diet which formerly "undernourished" them. They catch up on their development and become alert where they were once apathetic.

The custom of swaddling babies is undoubtedly related to the infant's need for tactile stimulation. In industrialized countries, swaddling is usually limited to wrapping newborn babies tightly in a receiving blanket. Many babies seem soothed by contact with the blanket even in hot weather. In traditional societies, swaddling goes much farther than the receiving blanket routine. The baby may be wrapped in long strips of cloth from feet to shoulders, so he becomes a rigid package like a little mummy. The swaddling cloths (which are rewrapped several times a day) may be left in place until the baby is a year old. The babies cry when the cloths are removed and seem soothed by their replacement. (The swaddled babies' motor development does not seem at all retarded by their physical restriction, incidentally.)

Breast-Feeding and Sucking

Before the twentieth century, breast-feeding was almost the only safe and convenient way to nourish a baby. The absence of refrigeration made cow's milk an excellent breeding place for bacteria. Without plastics or the vulcanization of rubber, good artificial nipples were difficult to create. Only the technological advances of the twentieth century made possible the controversy over the advantages and disadvantages of breast-feeding. In the early sixties, about twenty percent of American mothers breast-fed their newborn babies. From five to ten percent weaned the baby by three months; only one percent waited until the baby was two years old.

Researchers have not yet answered all the questions about either the physiological or the psychological characteristics of breast-feeding. In answer to the most recent questions about transmission of breast cancer through the mother's milk, it has been said that "the uncertain advantage to be gained by artificial feeding seems greatly outweighed by the nutritional, immunological, and psychological benefits of nursing at the breast" (Miller and Fraumeni, 1972, p. 645). In rare instances, formula feeding may involve dangers even beyond the well-known allergic reactions. A case has been reported in which a young baby died as a result of electrolyte imbalance when its semiliterate mother failed to dilute canned formula sufficiently (Coodin, Gabrielson, Addiego, 1971).

Breast-fed babies show a slightly lower weight gain in the early months of life, but it has been questioned whether the fastest rate of growth is necessarily the best for the baby's general development.

The often-claimed psychological benefits of breast-feeding are questionable. There are probably some aspects of development which are most readily fostered by nursing at the breast. Tactile contact between the mother's breast and the baby's skin is unavoidable. The mother's face is about eight inches from the baby's—the optimal distance for vision in the newborn—so the baby has an excellent chance to look at a human face and to practice visual fixation.

On the other hand, behavior problems in childhood do not seem to be associated in any simple way with the method of feeding in infancy (Heinstein, 1963). There is no clear benefit to behavior as a result of breast-feeding in itself for either boys or girls. Instead, there seems to be a complicated relationship among the warmth of the mother, the sex of the child, the method of feeding, and the frequency of childhood behavior problems. Girls with warm mothers were found to have fewer problems if they were exclusively bottle-fed. Boys with cold mothers had fewer problems of adjustment if they were nursed for a short time, while boys in better interpersonal environments behaved better if they were nursed for a longer period. The reverse was true for breast-fed girls; those with cold mothers benefitted from a longer nursing period, while warm mothers did better to nurse their daughters for a shorter time.

It has also been said that, "from the standpoint of psychological adjustment, even a little breast-feeding is better than none at all but that, if the mother does not plan to continue breast-feeding for at least a half-year or so, it might be better if she stops before her infant is much older than one month" (Caldwell, p. 29). "There are hints that gratification for the infant might be more closely related to the degree to which he can program his feeding regime than to whether he is fed from a breast or a bottle" (Caldwell, p. 41). In addition, "the practice of breast-feeding offered no guarantee of maternal sensitivity, nor did physical handling of the infant during feeding ensure emotional rapport and intimacy" (Caldwell, 1964, p. 65).

Thumb-Sucking

Newborn babies show a strong tendency to suck whatever comes into their mouths. The healthier and hungrier the baby, the stronger and more frequent the sucking. When the mother receives sedation during labor and birth the sucking rate and pressure of the newborn are affected for at least four days after birth (Kron et al., 1966).

Not all babies can get their thumbs into their mouths right away. Some may need a couple of months of development before they are capable of sucking their thumbs. But when they can do so, or when a pacifier is offered, nonnutritional sucking is likely to be carried out with enthusiasm. "It seems to be common in the first year for babies to seek extra sucking and to enjoy it. It does not necessarily appear to be a manifestation of unusual tension or frustration. Spock refers to this sucking as evidence of some unfulfilled need and urges mothers to examine their handling of the infant when this occurs. As a result, many conscientious young mothers feel guilty and bring their concerns to their physicians" (Brazelton, 1956, p. 400). Brazelton found that sixty-one out of seventy healthy babies began thumb-sucking sometime between birth and three months of age. The sucking activity became more intense up to about seven months and then began to decrease. Only four babies continued regular sucking after twelve months and only two continued beyond two years. Sucking on thumb or pacifier reduces general motor activity and may serve to provide the baby with some physical rest. Sucking also reduces the frequency of eye movement, which may help cut down the stimulation the baby receives from the outside world. The sucking baby, motionless and glazed of eye, does indeed appear withdrawn from the world. This look is unfortunately highly annoying to some adults, who do not appreciate that babies too sometimes need to rest without sleeping.

Is thumb-sucking related to feeding experiences? It might be that a baby who does not get to suck much while feeding may need extra sucking at other times; or, on the other hand, it might be that a baby who does little sucking will not develop an interest in sucking.

Yarrow (1954) studied sixty-six children in an attempt to answer questions. He found that babies who were breast-fed for more than six months show less severe and less prolonged thumb-sucking than those who had little or no breast-feeding. He also noted that the children who had the shortest feeding times in the early months were most likely to be severe thumb-suckers later on.

Thumb-sucking before the permanent teeth come in does not appear to deform the palate or tooth alignment. "The teeth in young children may be readily displaced by pressures of various sorts, but, in general, the teeth displaced in this way are readily replaced or resume their original positions spontaneously when the pressures are released" (Bakwin, 1948, p. 99).

Illness and Surgery

Serious illness, surgery, or hospitalization are important matters indeed to young children. Unfortunately, many pediatricians brush off parental concerns on these issues with the statement that children adapt very well to the hospital. The fact of the matter is that children may or may not adapt well to hospital routine, and that the chances of some subsequent distress are quite considerable.

The study of children's anxiety about medical treatment has led to the conclusion that "even a minor procedure such as stitch removal, if it is perceived as stressful by the child, can evoke an adrenocortical response" indicating anxiety and distress (Barnes et al., 1972, p. 259). Anesthesia is a procedure which is particular disturbing to children, but their fear can be lessened by having a parent present, discussing the procedure beforehand, and by allowing the child to "help" by holding the ether mask (Bothe and Galston, 1972).

For children as well as for adults, honest discussion and preparation before surgery helps the patient cope with pain and discomfort later. People who have been told that there will be no pain after surgery are much more distressed by their inevitable discomfort than those who have been told honestly that there will be some pain when they wake up. The worst thing one can do to a child going into surgery is to tell him he is going to a party. When such bald-faced lies have been told, the child must cope not only with his own bodily distress but also with the insight that he cannot believe or trust his own parents.

Reactions to minor illness improve with age. Children of two or three tend to cling and whine, while four-year-olds are much less demanding (Mattson and Weisberg, 1970). Reactions to hospitalization are a more complicated matter. In the young baby, distress over hospitalization is largely in reaction to separation from the mother. Disturbances such as increased anxiety after separation can occur as early as four months of age. As children get older and understand more of the situation, fears about what may happen to their bodies are added to the effects of separation. "Anxieties about bodily integrity provoked by . . . medical measures seemed most intense among . . . four- to six-year-old boys" (Yarrow, 1964, p. 113).

Distress during and after hospitalization is most commonly indicated by changed attitudes toward the mother. There is a simultaneous increase in dependency on the mother and in expression of hostility toward her. The child is afraid of losing the mother, but is angry at her for hospitalizing him, since he feels she is powerful enough to have prevented it if she wanted to. He tells her, "I don't want to live with you any more. I wish you weren't my mommy. I'm going to tell the nurse to call you and tell you not to visit me," and soon afterwards apologizes or asks for special attention and babying.

Much of the disturbance caused by hospitalization can be prevented if the hospital has a "care-by-parent" unit. Fifteen years ago, the British Ministry of Health recommended that all mothers of children under five stay with them in the hospital; parental care was considered so important that the National Health plan was required to pay for the mother's food and accommodations (Wessel and LaCamera, 1969). One English researcher has commented on this arrangement:

> Not all illnesses will be suited to this nursing, but the majority of all children under the age of 3 derive benefit from it. The mother lives in the same room with her child. She needs little

or no off-duty time, because the sleep requirements of a mother fall near to zero when her own child is acutely ill. She feeds the child; she tends the child; she keeps it in its most comfortable posture, whether on its pillow or on her knee. The sister and nurse are at hand to help and to administer technical treatment to the child. The advantages of the system are fourfold. It is an advantage to the child. It is an advantage to the mother, for to have undergone this experience and to have felt that she has been responsible for her own child's recovery establishes a relationship with her child and confidence in herself which bodes well for the future. It is an advantage to the nurses, who learn much by contact with the best of these women, not only about the handling of a child but about life itself. It is an advantage to the other children in the ward, for whose care more nursing time is liberated. (Wessel and LaCamera, 1969, p. 304).

The care-by-parent unit has also been estimated to be cheaper to run (James and Wheeler, 1969). Given these facts, it is difficult to understand why, in many sections of the United States, parents must travel long distances to find a hospital which will allow them unlimited visiting time with their child. Even if they do find such a place, they will usually have to sleep sitting in a chair or on the floor and will slip out to McDonald's for hurried meals.

Developing Defense Mechanisms

The two-year-old may be as open and transparent about his feelings as one could possibly want. He confides all sorts of things which an adult would be embarrassed to tell about himself. The little boy expresses his jealousy of his father's "great big penis," the little girl explains how angry she is about the new baby. Two-year-olds do not feel they should try to be brave. They are unashamedly afraid of the dark, the closet, the big dog.

Modern parents of a two-year-old may feel very pleased with the ease of their child's communication. They look forward to years of easy understanding, with constant improvement as the child's verbal abilities develop. But they do not reckon on a development which is soon to come.

At age three, or four, the transparency of the two-year-old will give way to an inscrutable refusal to discuss matters laden with emotion. The formerly open, communicative child now tells his parents that he "doesn't want to talk about it," or cries, or becomes angry, when they try to broach emotional subjects. No one has offended or mishandled him—he has simply matured to the point where he is developing *defense mechanisms*.

The defense mechanisms are ways of acting which protect a person from feelings of anxiety and fear of punishment. Rather than consciously being aware of his emotions, he protects himself against them by doing or thinking other things. The development of defense mechanisms is perfectly normal and in fact desirable for everyone, for they save us much distress and concern over matters which we cannot change.

Three defense mechanisms which seem common among preschoolers are *regression, denial,* and *rationalization*. Regression is a return to more infantile behavior under stress. The child deals with his anxiety by sucking his thumb, drinking from a bottle, or wetting his bed, though he had given up such babyish activities before the stressful situation occurred. He is not trying to get attention (though he may get more than he expected). His return to babyhood is one way of coping with fear.

Denial is a means of defense against fear in which the child refuses to admit that the anxiety-producing situation exists at all. Superficially, denial may appear to be lying or simple stupidity, but in fact it serves the purpose of keeping fear out of consciousness. A child is using denial when he insists that his parents will be home for supper even though he has been told quite clearly that they are going on vacation for a week.

Rationalization involves elaborate explanation of mistakes or of desires which adults do not want to gratify. The energy put into the reasoning process helps keep the genuine feelings of anger and fear of punishment out of conscious awareness. Rationalization often seems to involve statements beginning, "*Well,* Mommy, I had to . ." or "*Well,* Mommy, it just fell over and you shouldn't have left it there. . . ."

It is important to realize that denial and rationalization are not deliberate lies or evasions. They are methods of dealing with a situation which has become too much for the child to cope with.

Sleep Problems

Many parents have sleep problems, but most children do not, at least not in the strict sense of the term. The restless, broken

sleep, with a number of awakenings each night, which charac-
terizes many children's rest, is often due simply to immaturity. But
it can be a genuine problem for parents, who sometimes feel they
will go mad if they don't get a couple of nights of unbroken sleep.

Young babies tend to have fussy periods in the early morning
and also in the late evening, with a peak of fussiness occurring at
about six weeks of age. The most common times for ten-week-olds
to fuss are 6 to 12 A.M. and 5 to 11 P.M. (Brazelton, 1962).
Though parents sometimes hope that a night feeding of cereal will
get the baby to sleep through to a reasonable hour, several studies
have "failed to confirm the belief that an infant fed solid food in
the evening is more likely to sleep through the night than one who
is given liquid diet alone" (Guthrie, 1966, p. 879).

About seventy percent of babies sleep through the night by
the time they are three months old. By six months, another thirteen
percent have begun to sleep from about midnight to early morning. "Ten percent never sleep uninterruptedly during the first
year" (Anders, 1975, p. 23). Even among the infants who have begun to sleep through, about fifty percent have some time between
five and nine months when they begin to wake up again. This may
be the result of new beds or bedrooms, separations, or other minor
incidents.

Children between twelve and eighteen months are more likely
to resist falling asleep. Sleep is reacted to as a form of separation,
and responded to with anxiety. To help them go to sleep, children
of this age often need bedtime rituals and "security" blankets or
toys.

Two-year-olds tend to have sleep problems which center
around frightening dreams. The explanation that "it was just a
dream" is no comfort to them, because they think that dreams are
things which come into the bedroom and which could be seen by
anyone in the room.

According to Anders, "it is rare to find a child in the three-
to-five-year age group who is not experiencing some difficulty
about sleep, whether it be tardiness in falling asleep, night
wakening, nightmares, projective fears of ghosts and wild animals,
inability to sleep alone or in the dark, or ritualistic pre-sleep be-

havior. Most of these disturbances are transient" (p. 23). The child, so busy and apparently happy during the day, shows at night the stress he experiences from the demands of socialization.

Several disturbances of sleep can be described. Persistent sleepwalking occurs in between one percent and six percent of all people. Boys are more likely than girls to sleepwalk, though fifteen percent of all children between age five and twelve are said to have walked in their sleep at least once. Here is the typical sleepwalking sequence. A body movement is followed by the subject abruptly sitting upright in bed; the eyes are open, glassy, and appear "unseeing"; the subject may or may not actually get up and leave the bed; doors and drawers may be opened, furniture skirted. The movements are clumsy but collisions and actual physical injury are generally avoided. Efforts to communicate with the sleepwalker may elicit mumbled and slurred speech with monosyllabic answers that are poorly related to the question. Occasionally spontaneous somniloquy is observed. The total duration of the episode may range from fifteen to thirty seconds when sitting in bed, to five to thirty minutes or more when actual walking occurs. Walking generally ends with the child returning to his bed to sleep. There is amnesia for the event upon awakening. Severe sleep walkers may have episodes one to four times weekly.

"Night terror," or *pavor nocturnus,* is a disorder which superficially resembles a severe nightmare. The difference is that the child remembers a nightmare but has no recollection of the night terror. In *pavor nocturnus,* the child suddenly sits upright in bed and screams. He appears to be staring at an imaginary object, breathes heavily, often perspires, and is in obvious distress. He is usually inconsolable for ten minutes or more, then finally relaxes and returns to sleep. Immediate dream recall is fragmentary, if present at all, and in the morning there is amnesia for the attack. Though seen in older children and adults, night terrors are most common in the preschool age group.

Night terrors do not usually occur frequently. If they do, however, they can be treated with drugs, as can frequent sleepwalking.

Little girls sometimes awaken at night crying and complaining of pain in the vagina or urethra. This may be caused by migration of pinworms, and is cured by getting rid of the worms (Levin, 1969).

Aggression

Some hostile, angry, or destructive behavior is bound to occur in the life of any normal child. When frustrated, corrected, or punished, most children will respond on occasion by attacking the person who is the apparent source of their distress. Sometimes the child's attack is quite startling in its vigor and seriousness; toddlers are seen to try to strangle or gouge eyes when they have never themselves been exposed to anything stronger than a mild smack on the bottom.

Every parent has to make a decision, based on personal values, about the amount of aggressiveness desirable in a child (and, later, in the adult he will become). Few parents wish to suppress aggression completely. Peaceful though they may be in their own households, they feel distressed if their child does not respond in kind to another child's attack. Almost everyone wants a child who can defend himself. The question is rarely one of complete suppression of aggressiveness. Instead, people try to limit the objects of aggression (not the baby; not the cat or dog; not the parents themselves) or the means of aggression (hitting may be acceptable, but biting or the use of weapons may not).

There is a good deal of evidence that complete suppression of conscious feelings and actions of aggressiveness is a bad idea. People whose angry feelings have been buried too deeply are capable of losing all control when pushed too far, and committing serious acts of aggression. In newspaper stories about mass murders, neighbors of the murderer are often quoted as saying that the killer was "such a good boy," quiet, an honor student, never argued, and so on. The neighbors are surprised, but in fact it is the boys who are too good, too quiet, too cooperative, who crack up and kill their entire families. People need to have some socially acceptable means of expressing anger, or they learn only to suppress their impulses and not to control them.

On the other hand, poor control of aggressive impulses may lead to constant quarreling and fighting over trivial disagreements.

People who express anger too readily may also find themselves in trouble.

What determines a child's expression of aggression? Several factors in his experience and environment are important.

Modeling   The aggressive aspects of a child's behavior depend to a considerable extent on the ways he sees his parents act. Children learn from observation how people ought to behave, and what they observe their parents doing is more important than anything else they see. They do as the parents do, and not as they say. Thus, a child who is brought up in a quarrelsome environment is likely to show more impulsive anger than one who never sees the open expression of hostility.

Punishment experiences   A child who receives a good deal of physical punishment is more likely to be physically aggressive than one whose punishment involves loss of approval, isolation from the family, and fear that he will lose his parents' love.

Social roles   Social approval or disapproval of particular expressions of anger help determine the ways in which a child shows aggression. For instance, by the time they start school, girls show more verbal aggression, while boys show both physical and verbal aggression.

Frustration   A child who meets many severe frustrations—inadequate nutrition, poor clothing, lack of sleep—is more likely to be unduly aggressive than one whose basic needs are satisfied.

In one study of adult murderers (Palmer, 1960), it appeared that murderers experience childhoods which are full of pain and frustration. A large number of the murderers had experienced difficult births, congenital deformities, birth injuries, serious operations and injuries. They were unusually likely to have been unwanted children and to have been fed and toilet trained rigidly.

Equilibrium and Disequilibrium

To realize the natural emotional cycles of young children helps the adult to deal with them. Children really do "go through stages," and their behavior at any time does not necessarily tell you how they will be acting 6 months from then. Periods of equilibrium, in which the child is happy, active, and cooperative, alternate with periods of disequilibrium, when nothing is accomplished easily and parents ask themselves whether any boarding schools take three-year-olds. These transitions of mood and behavior can be expected every 6 months or so from eighteen months to about six years of age. The alternating periods are part of a child's natural development. The bad periods cannot be completely erased by any amount of careful handling. Parents and teachers must simply bite the bullet and look forward to the time when the next period of equilibrium will arrive.

Boys and girls have somewhat different patterns of equilibrium and disequilibrium. Figure 12 shows the differences.

Figure 12.

Changes in irritability with age. (From E. Hurlock, *Developmental Psychology*, p. 364. Copyright © 1968. Used with permission of McGraw-Hill Book Co.)

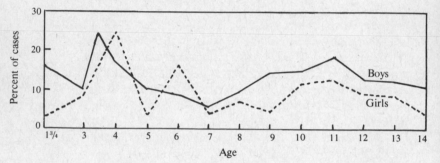

Boys have a peak of irritability at about three and a half, while girls peak a bit later. The boys have a gradual reduction in irritability and then a slow rise till the time of puberty, while girls show an unusually "good" period at about five, followed by another peak of irritability at six.

Discipline Techniques and Children's Behavior

There are many variations in the disciplinary techniques which parents use. Some of these differences occur because ethnic groups and social classes vary in their approaches to child rearing. Parental personality differences also help determine a family's disciplinary habits. The type of discipline employed, whatever its cause, seems to have a powerful influence on behavior the children display both in their early years and also later in life.

The disciplinary atmosphere of a home can be analyzed into two factors: warmth versus hostility, and permissiveness versus restrictiveness (Becker, 1964, p. 198). Warm parents are accepting, approving, and affectionate, while hostile parents are rejecting, critical, and cold. Permissive parents insist on relatively little conformity to rules, while restrictive parents have a long list of things their children must or must not do. Each of these qualities affects the children not only in itself but also in interaction with one of the others.

The warm, affectionate, but rule-conscious and restrictive, home produces children who conform well to rules but who do not take much initiative. They are characterized as submissive, dependent, polite, neat, obedient, unaggressive, unfriendly, and uncreative.

The affectionate home where children are not asked to conform excessively tends to produce children who are characterized as active, outgoing, creative, independent, and friendly.

The home where parents are rejecting and where conformity is stressed tends to produce children who have "neurotic" problems; who quarrel and are shy with their peers; who are socially withdrawn.

When parents are hostile and do not exert much discipline, the children tend to be delinquent, noncompliant, and aggressive.

In looking at discipline techniques we can also consider parental punitiveness, the use of psychological punishment, inconsistency of discipline, the effect of too much discipline, and the effect of hostility between parent and child (Becker, 1964).

When parents consistently use frequent punishment, the children tend to be highly aggressive during the early years of childhood. But groups of people among whom both parents are consistently punitive are also the groups which show the lowest crime rates in later life.

Psychological, rather than physical, punishment may be used in several different ways. So-called *induction techniques* of punishment involve "insisting on restitution or apology, asking why he did that, explaining to the child why it was wrong, or not punishing if the child shows recognition that he has done wrong" (Becker, p. 183). These techniques seem to encourage the child to take responsibility for his actions by giving him unpleasant feelings about misbehavior even in the absence of an external threat. Induction techniques seem best suited to produce conformity to social rules, since breaking the social rule does not necessarily have bad consequences unless one is caught. *Sensitization techniques,* on the other hand, might work best with rules involving natural dangers, like a prohibition against playing ball in the street. They aim at "inhibiting the child's unacceptable behavior by focusing on the painful consequences" (Becker, p. 183). *Love-oriented punishment* threatens the child with loss of love and approval unless he mends his ways, but may be effective only when there is a real awareness that enough love exists for its loss to matter.

When parents do not apply punishment in similar ways, problems develop. Boys whose parents differ in the consistency of their punishment are more aggressive than if both parents were punitive or if both were nonpunitive.

A sense of responsibility seems to develop better when discipline is not excessively strong. However, boys seem to benefit from stricter discipline than girls can deal with. When the authority of the father is strong, a sense of responsibility is encouraged in boys but impeded in girls.

Bickering and conflict between parents and children can be unpleasant for all concerned and is certainly nerve-racking for parents, who find life with obedient children much more pleasant. But children may learn some important skills from open hostilities. "It is not yet clear to what degree a certain amount of openly hostile interaction between parent and child may actually facilitate the child's ability to cope with the realities of independent living in our society. . . . Acceptance of boys by their peers in our culture requires an ability to react to provoked attack by an adequate counter-attack. Disciplinary procedures, which strongly inhibit or fail to provide models for such behavior, could foster adjustment problems for boys with their peers" (Becker, p. 203).

The specific approach used by parents in exerting discipline may also help determine its effect, as may general attitudes toward the child. One study examined the speech patterns of mothers of normal children as compared to those of mothers of disturbed children. The former spoke more assertively to their children when they made statements of approval or disapproval than when they spoke of neutral topics. The mothers of disturbed children reversed the situation; they were less assertive when telling their children something was good or bad than when talking about the weather (Bugental and Love, 1975). In another study, both normal and deviant children were found to be more likely to act bad if others were told they were bad, but no more likely to be good if they were presented as good (Lobitz and Johnson, 1975).

Symptoms of Disturbance

Diagnosis is a dangerous game. Children who receive a diagnostic label early in life may find it very hard to escape, no matter how inaccurate the label may be. The immature two-year-old, youngest at his day-care center, runs around a lot, and his teacher tells his mother he is "hyperactive." An eight-year-old's school files bear the notations that he is "homicidal" and has "homosexual tendencies"; on investigation these remarks appear to be based on his possession of a pocketknife and an untidy consumption of candy which his teacher perceived as lipstick on his mouth. These labels may remain in the children's records and reputations for years.

In applying labels, people should remember that there is no wide gulf between normality and abnormality. All normal children may at certain times display behavior which is also shown by disturbed children. In addition, we should remain aware that behavior which is a nuisance to adults is not necessarily disturbed behavior.

There are two major categories in which we might class childhood emotional disturbances: behavior problems which make it difficult for the child to learn and develop, and problems which are simply objectionable to adults while the individual is a child, and which are predictive of unacceptable behavior in later life. In the first category are such disturbances as hyperkinesis and autism, while the second category includes fire-setting, cruelty to animals, and poor impulse control.

Hyperkinesis is a disorder which involves abnormally high activity levels, poor concentration, short attention span, and consequent learning difficulties. It is thought to result from minimal brain damage caused by difficulties at birth. Diagnosis of hyperkinesis requires considerable skill and training, especially since almost all children are overactive by adult standards. Many methods of treatment have been suggested—a calm, nonstimulating environment; a highly stimulating environment; vitamin therapy; exclusion of artificial additives from the diet; the use of drugs. Paradoxically, the drugs used in treating hyperkinetic children act as stimulants for most people, but calm hyperactive behavior. Unfortunately, they also tend to suppress the production of growth hormone. In most patients, hyperkinesis disappears some time between age eight and age twenty-one (Menkes et al., 1967).

Autism is a disorder of behavior which begins early in life. The child is apparently happy, but is socially withdrawn. He does not smile and look at people or try to stay near them. He plays alone, with repetitive and stereotyped movements. Though his physical development is normal, he does not learn to speak. He may be very interested in music and numbers. The source of autism is questionable. More autistic children are boys; more are firstborn; they are likely to have highly intellectual, emotionally cold mothers. These factors seem to suggest that autism occurs as a result of early experience. However, it is also said that autistic children are different from the very beginning—that they never cuddle or snuggle. Treatment of autism is a difficult matter. Some success has been achieved through behavior modification.

Fire-setting and severe *cruelty to animals* are bothersome, but do not cause most adults to worry seriously about a child's future. They are, in fact, indicative of serious emotional problems which are likely to be expressed in antisocial ways during adulthood. Poor impulse control is shown in frequent tantrums and fits of temper after early childhood is past—a tantrum a week or more, after the age of five, for instance. Fire-setting, cruelty, and poor impulse control are commonly found in the childhoods of people who later commit violent crimes.

Breath-holding spells are an occasional problem which should not be regarded with extreme concern. In these spells, formally termed cyanotic and pallid infantile syncope, "the child may be frightened, hurt, or angered, cry vigorously for one or a few breaths; then hold his breath. After a few seconds, he becomes more or less cyanotic, loses consciousness, and falls limp. . . . The milder episodes are sufficiently common as to be regarded tolerantly by both doctors and parents" (Lombroso and Lerman, 1967, p. 563). The spells may be frequent and followed by prolonged unconsciousness. They may also include convulsions; the child may turn pale or blue. Sometimes only one cry or a gasp occurs at the beginning of the spell. About five percent of children have breath-holding spells. They are not related to epilepsy or mental deficiency and usually stop spontaneously before school age.

Chapter 5
Social Growth

Children in day care appear to remain physically and psychologically healthy, and learn some important social skills. Becoming toilet trained is a crucial skill which must be achieved before a child is a full member of his society. Although some behavioral differences between boys and girls are biological in background, learning of a socially approved sex role is an important task for children. Development of a moral code is another aspect of social growth.

Social Growth

A child's social development involves many factors. It depends partly on his social experiences, on his exposure to other people in large or small groups. The day-care experience and its potential benefit or harm are important related issues here.

Social growth also concerns the learning of conformity to society's many rules. Though it is sometimes seen as stifling, conformity eases social functioning by making certain decisions unnecessary. Guests do not have to decide, for instance, whether their hostess would prefer for them to eliminate in her toilet or in her washing machine. Children have their first real contact with social demands for conformity in the context of toilet training. Later, pressure is exerted so that the child will bring his behavior in line with his sex role. Throughout childhood, the individual matures in his ways of making normal judgments; he learns through trial and error what specific moral judgments are made by adults in his society.

Day Care and Development

For many children in the United States today, attendance at a day-care center is a crucial factor in social experience and development. Social changes in adult society have increased the demand for and use of formal, organized day-care facilities. Whether a mother works for professional satisfaction or because of economic necessity, she is likely to prefer an established day-care center over the hazards of the individual baby-sitter. More and more very young children thus find themselves spending most of their waking hours with a few adults and twenty or more other children, rather than living with a few brothers and sisters.

Twenty years ago, many child development researchers had serious reservations about day care. Little was known about the effects of attendance at day-care centers, because there were few in existence. But most workers in child development assumed that research on children in orphanages was relevant to the day-care situation. The development of institutionalized babies and toddlers was known to suffer serious disturbance. Babies who were taken from their mothers and cared for in orphanages failed to thrive or even died, apparently as a result of lack of stimulation and attention. Toddlers sometimes stopped growing when neglected or institutionalized; this syndrome, called "deprivation dwarfism," showed real physical changes resulting from a lack of mothering. These facts made child development workers hesitate to encourage the development of day-care programs.

Day care grew, nonetheless, under the social pressures of the 1960s. And, as time went on, it became clear that the fears of earlier days were unjustified. Day care is in no way equivalent to institutionalization.

The acceptability of day care as a way of life for preschoolers first became evident in countries other than the United States. The *kibbutz* situation in Israel has long employed a day-care-like child-rearing method. *Kibbutz* children are placed in a special infants' house some time before the fifth day of life. From that time on, they are cared for primarily by professional child-care workers. The mother of a breast-fed baby will visit several times a day to nurse the infant, but virtually all the rest of the baby's care is provided by the caretaker—who may have ten to twenty other babies to care for at the same time. The baby may go for brief periods to visit the parents' room after it is six months old, but it is very unlikely that the family will be united for more than an hour each day. The baby thus receives very little attention other than through feeding and other physical care. "Mothering" does not exist in the traditional sense of cuddling, comforting, and encouraging attachment. The *kibbutz* members deliberately set out to discourage the babies from becoming attached to their parents or to individual caretakers; the babies are expected to become attached and committed to the *kibbutz* group as a whole, and especially to their age-mates.

The *kibbutz* situation sounds bizarre in comparison to American family life. Even American day care is tame when compared to life in the infants' house. Most of us would predict intuitively that the *kibbutz* babies would grow up severely disturbed. The child development researchers of the 1950s would certainly have said so. But the fact is that the children of the *kibbutz* grow up happy and healthy. As it was planned that they should do, they make their emotional commitments to the other children in their age group. They are upset when separated from the other children—not when their parents go home or when a new caretaker comes on duty.

China provides another example of the success of group child care. A large proportion of Chinese babies today accompany their mothers to a "nursing room" in the mother's place of work. There babies over the age of fifty-six days are cared for by "aunties" except for the two periods each day when their mothers come in to nurse them. In one nursing room, described by Ruth Sidel (1973), four "aunties" cared for twenty-seven babies ranging in age from fifty-six days to eighteen months. The caretakers wheeled the babies around in carriages when they cried, since there were too many babies to pick up. When the children reach walking age, they are not allowed to walk in the nursery room, since it is too crowded with cribs and since the "aunties" feel the floor is too dirty. They are prevented from sucking their fingers, which the "aunties" also consider dirty. In spite of their apparent lack of stimulation and mothering, the nursing room babies follow a developmental schedule very similar to that of American babies.

For children over the age of eighteen months, Chinese cities even offer a few twenty-four-hour nurseries. (The major reason the children are not placed in a boarding nursery at an earlier age is that virtually all Chinese babies are breast-fed until eighteen months.) The Chinese actually feel that children progress more quickly in the boarding nursery, where they are not spoiled by their grandparents.

The evidence from Israel and China suggests that communal child rearing can be very successful. More recent research in the United States has led to the same conclusion.

Bettye Caldwell has asked the question, "Can children have a quality life in day care?" (in Coopersmith and Feldman, 1974). Her answers to this question are based on a variety of research findings, which will be summarized here.

1. "A full range of experiences will be encountered by children in day care; one can no more speak of day care in the singular than one can of 'school' " (p. 89). In other words, day-care centers vary widely in the formats of their programs, the training their teachers have received, their physical setups, and so on. There is no single meaning for the term "day care."

2. "Children in day care develop motivationally and in terms of skills considered adaptive in today's world" (p. 89). No intellectual loss occurs as a result of separation from the family during the day.

3. "Children in day care can be kept healthy" (p. 91). In high-quality day-care programs there may be a slight increase in the number of colds for children under 1 year of age, but after that there is little difference in the number of illnesses suffered by day-care and by home-reared children.

4. "Children in day care do not lose their attachment to their mothers" (p. 92). Children who have been in day care since a time prior to their first birthday have been found to be no less attached to their mothers than children reared at home.

5. "Young children in day care do not necessarily become emotionally disturbed" (p. 94). Concern has often been expressed about the emotional development of children placed in day care before the age of three. It now appears that relatively good adjustment occurs whether the child was under three or over three when started in day care.

6. "Children in day care develop a sense of community" (p. 94). Day-care children develop a deep concern for each other's rights and needs, and behave as if they were a large family of brothers and sisters. Such a sense of community is much less likely to develop in children reared at home, whose major contacts may be with one or two children, or solely with adults.

Research other than that summarized by Caldwell is generally in agreement with the statements given above, but some interesting details and exceptions may be added.

For instance, some writers on this subject feel that the age at which a child may go into day care or nursery school depends on the individual child. "Individual differences in rates of development and in temperament must also be considered. The active outgoing child may find the nursery a challenge and an opportunity, or he may find the degree of social stimulation so great as to be overtiring. A more passive, less outgoing child, in a similar situation, might make an easier adjustment because he is less responsive to the social stimulation" (Swift, p. 272).

In addition, some periods during the child's life may be better than others for the initiation of day care. The period between six and nine months is an especially sensitive time for the attachment between mother and child, and is thus a poor time for changing caretakers. The time around the second birthday, when language skills are being consolidated, may be another bad time for entering day care (Howell, 1973). Periods of negativism in early childhood, which occur in all children (in girls, with a peak at about eighteen months; in boys, with a peak at about thirty months), might create problems by giving parents the impression that day care has caused the child's negativism.

A possible increase in aggressiveness and reluctance to accept adult values have been suggested as a result of day care.

The absence of male influence in the average day-care center gives a real disadvantage in comparison to the traditional nuclear family. Both boys and girls in day care are at an age where sex-role identification is helped by contact with adults of both sexes. "Nursery schools, kindergartens, and elementary schools would have a greater positive influence on children if more male teachers were available" (Biller, 1971, p. 131). Of course, the traditional nuclear family seems to be becoming a thing of the past, and many children in day care would have no greater contact with adult males if they stayed at home.

In judging the effect of any specific day-care center, it should be remembered that day-care children develop a powerful emotional commitment to the other children in their center. Like the children of the *kibbutz,* day-care children have a group attachment which may well transcend their attachment to their teachers. For this reason, it is important that a day-care center have a reasonably consistent population of children. There will naturally be some turnover, as children move away or enter kindergarten, but any individual child should have some age-mates whose presence is reliable enough to allow the development of an attachment. This is especially important if a child has started in day care before six months of age, in which case he may not have established a very strong attachment to his mother.

Toilet Training

Toilet training is a process which is both physiological and social in nature. Its physiological character has to do with the need for maturation of the nervous system before elimination comes under voluntary control. Since the development of the nervous system proceeds from the head end to the foot end, the mouth and hands can be controlled voluntarily earlier than the lower parts of the body. The legs and the sphincter muscles of bowels and bladder are among the last parts to achieve voluntary control. Before such control is achieved, no amount of effort can produce genuine toilet training.

When parents claim that a child was "trained" at the age of nine or ten months, it usually turns out that the mother has trained herself to anticipate the child's needs and to place it on the pot as the appropriate time approaches. Years ago, it was customary to start "training" by placing the child on the pot when it was a month old. If this method was carefully carried out, the child could be expected to be trained by eighteen or nineteen months. Today, people start the process at sixteen months, and the child is trained by eighteen or nineteen months.

The best index of a child's physiological readiness for toilet training is steady walking. A child who walks may not yet be ready for elimination training for emotional or intellectual reasons, but a healthy child who does not yet walk is not ready for reasons of physiological maturation.

The social aspect of elimination training is a very important one. Every society has some form of elimination training. Some forms are very strict, some rather casual, but in no case is the child simply expected to control his elimination without being taught. He is shown specifically what to do and is told to imitate his parents or siblings. (There may be special cultural ways of dealing with the training period; we have training pants; the Chinese use special open-backed pants which the child does not need to pull down; the Balinese have household dogs which clean up any messes made by nude toddlers.) But he is always told *something*. Human beings apparently need special training to learn to control elimination. The skill does not occur spontaneously, and if the child gets too old (say, four or more) before training is begun, elimination control becomes very hard to establish. Perhaps if we were related to predatory animals, who hide their feces, rather than to apes, who foul their own nests, matters would be simpler.

The control of elimination is the first serious demand which society makes on the child. For the first time, he is asked to conform, to give up immediate satisfaction of his needs, and, indeed, to believe that conformity is good and desirable. No wonder toilet training can become a battleground between parent and child—it is a situation which represents all the pressures toward and against socialization.

Readiness for elimination training increases with age, but the relationship between age and ease of training is not a simple one. Certain stages in the child's development make toilet training difficult. For instance, at some ages children are very active and find it almost impossible to sit down long enough to use a toilet or potty chair. Or, if he becomes afraid of the water going down the drain in the bathtub, he may have a similar fear of the toilet.

Gesell and Ilg (1943) suggested that children alternate between a powerful tendency to *inhibition* and a powerful tendency to *release,* until they manage to get good voluntary control over both. Elimination control requires both of these mechanisms: inhibition of elimination until the proper time and place, and release of the function within a reasonable time after the toilet is reached. Children in an inhibition period may avoid accidents completely, but sit on the toilet indefinitely without releasing—or lose control and release as soon as their clothes are back on. Children in a release period seem to have a training relapse and fail to get to the bathroom on time.

One indication of readiness for toilet training is the child's communication that elimination is about to occur or has just occurred. Many children have a word, gesture, or expression which communicates their needs to adults. Others have a negative form of communication: they hide when they feel the need to eliminate. They may go behind a chair if indoors, or under a bush or low tree if outdoors. If the mother searches for them, they may call out, "Mommy, go 'way!"

What if a child does not imitate at once, and uses no form of communication? What if he shows no discomfort when his diaper is wet or soiled? No single practical prescription will be appropriate for every child. But some flexibility and a logical analysis of the task at hand may help.

First, elimination training may be divided into a series of necessary but separate steps:

1. Awareness by the child of physical pressures which warn of approaching elimination.
2. Communication to an adult that help is needed.
3. Inhibition of elimination while the bathroom is reached, clothes are removed, and so on.
4. Release of elimination in response to a verbal command, or to the feeling of the toilet or potty against the body.

These steps will not take place simultaneously. *However, as long as one or more are present and can be rewarded, toilet training is continuing to advance.* The child may be perfectly aware of internal pressure, but make no communication, or he may communicate but be unable to inhibit elimination until he reaches the toilet. He may be able to inhibit, but unable to release when the time comes. If the problem is the last, the physical situation itself may need to be changed. Children often become trained for one toilet or potty, but cannot release in a strange place. If this is the case, taking along a child's toilet seat or his potty when visiting may be helpful. A child may also be afraid of the toilet because he feels unstable and fears falling in. A low potty chair may be much better accepted in this case. (One disadvantage of the usual American potty chair is that it comes apart too easily in the hands of the toddler who wants to empty the pot into the toilet. A European one-piece pot is better—or, for that matter, a dog-food dish with a weighted bottom works quite well.)

What if a child balks at the use of any container at all? He can be praised for telling the parent and waiting until he gets to the bathroom, and then allowed to squat over a sheet of newspaper. Or, in summer, if the neighbors are sufficiently tolerant, he can go outdoors. Though these solutions are temporary, they allow the child to be praised and to feel pleased with himself. When the parent insists that all four steps must be perfect before any reward is given, the situation becomes hostile and frustrating for everyone involved.

When a child appears particularly hard to train, it has been suggested that extra liquids be given in order to increase the frequency of experience of urination. A special potty chair which gives a musical signal when urination occurs (Star Tinkle, Nursery Training Devices, Inc., Concord, California) is also recommended (Foxx and Azrin, 1973).

In a study of the elimination habits of two-and-a-half-year-old children, some information was gathered on frequencies of urination and defecation (Roberts and Schoellkopp, 1951, a, b). About eighty percent of children of this age urinate every two or three hours during the day. About ten percent of the girls and about 5 percent of the boys went four hours or more between urinations, while ten percent of the girls and eight percent of the boys urinated every hour or so. About forty percent of the children still sometimes wet themselves during the day, and a slightly larger proportion still wet the bed at night. About fifteen percent wet the bed at naptime. Almost seventy percent of the girls were dry during the day, as compared to fifty percent of the boys.

Bowel patterns were investigated in the same study. In a group of 783 two-and-a-half-year-old children, about sixty percent had one bowel movement per day, while ten percent moved their bowels several times every day. About four percent had a movement every other day, or less frequently. About fifty percent of the children had their movements at about the same time each day, the other fifty percent being unpredictable. Almost ninety percent of the children in this study had reliable bowel control. About twice as many boys as girls had bowel-training problems.

Taking responsibility for getting to the toilet is one aspect of toilet training. This can be the responsibility of the mother, of the child, or a shared responsibility. For both bowel and urination training, mothers tend to take responsibility more often for their sons than for their daughters. "One wonders if it is because boys actually need more help than girls or if there is a psychologic factor operating that encourages mothers to keep their boys more dependent on them. Perhaps mothers let girls at this age take more initiative than boys in managing their toileting needs. Perhaps girls are more compliant with their mothers than are boys, or it may be that mothers are more fastidious about girls and help them to be clean earlier than boys, so that by the age of thirty months girls are further advanced than are boys" (Roberts and Schoellkopf, 1951a, p. 146).

Frequency of urination has some association with the ability to stay dry. The infrequent urinaters in this study were more likely to be dry than wet.

Picking the child up and taking him to the toilet during the night is often thought of as a way to encourage keeping dry at night. But over forty percent of the children in this study who were picked up at night continued to wet the bed nonetheless. Over fifty percent who were *not* picked up did not wet the bed. "It seems valid to conclude that the taking up of these children aged two-and-a-half years during the night was only a moderately successful procedure in keeping them dry" (Roberts and Schoellkopf, p. 151).

Staying dry at night usually takes longer than daytime training. Some fifty percent of children are dry at night by age two; seventy-five percent are dry by three; and ninety percent sleep dry by age five. More boys than girls wet the bed after age five (Pringle, Butler, and Davis, 1966).

The common bed-wetting of early childhood should not really be considered a problem in need of therapy until after age five or so. When bed-wetting appears as a problem, common sense may in some cases indicate the appropriate therapy. Does the bathroom light need to be left on? Has the child been scolded for wandering in the night so he thinks he must stay in bed, however urgent his need? In these cases, he may be awake when he urinates, but too afraid to get up.

In real enuresis, on the other hand, the child does not awaken as his bladder becomes distended, and urination occurs while he is still sleeping. When this condition is present, several forms of professional therapy have been used. (1) One involves surgery to enlarge a constricted urethra, which may be present in some cases. (2) Another method uses the drug imipramine, which causes changes in sleep rhythms. (3) There are also devices which allow conditioning of awakening in response to bladder distention. A bladder conditioning device consists of a bell and a pad on which the child lies. When a few drops of urine wet the pad, an electrical circuit is closed, and a very weak electric current passes along a wire and rings the bell, awakening the child. (Note carefully—*no electric shock is involved here!* The current is too weak to be felt.) After several nights, the feeling of the full bladder comes to act as a signal that the bell will soon ring, and the child awakens before urination begins. Such conditioning devices can be bought without a prescription, but they should be used only under supervision, since the mild electric current can produce skin ulcers in the area which contacts the pad.

Some workers in the therapy of enuresis feel that the approaches described above do not work as well as methods which enlist the child as an active helper. Two such methods have been suggested (Marshall, Marshall, and Lyon, 1973). (1) *Shaping* of dryness may be carried out with the help of an alarm clock (see Chapter 8 for a more detailed description of shaping). If the child rarely gets through an entire dry night, he will rarely be rewarded if we insist on a whole dry night as our goal. However, he can be rewarded much more frequently for a number of dry *hours* each night. First, the child must be observed in order to find how many hours in bed pass before he urinates. An alarm clock may then be set for a period slightly *shorter* than the usual dry period. When it rings, the child is awakened, praised, rewarded, and taken to the bathroom. After a few nights of this, the clock is set for a slightly later time, and so on, until the child begins to awaken by himself or until the whole night is spent dry.

(2) A second method in which the child can participate actively is *sensation awareness training.* One cause of enuresis may be poor sensitivity to the fullness of the bladder. In this form of training, the child is asked during the day to postpone urination as long as possible, to concentrate on the feeling, and then to measure the amount of urine finally produced. The encouragement and help of an adult are essential here.

Sex-Role Development

Society demands that each individual act like either a male or female. People expect to recognize every human being as belonging to one or the other sex, and they feel profoundly uneasy when someone's behavior is ambiguous. Yet the details of male or female behavior—clothing, language, hobbies—differ greatly from culture to culture. Thus each baby must learn, as it grows up, the behavior its culture accepts as right for its biological sex.

Boy and girl infants differ somewhat in their basic behavior and development. These differences are biological rather than learned. But the biological differences are not great enough to explain the tremendous differences in behavior and personality between adult men and women. To explain these, we need to look at differences in the way adults treat little boys and little girls.

Mothers, no matter how fair they try to be, give different kinds of attention to their infant sons and daughters. Middle-class American mothers spend more time talking to their girl babies than to their boys—perhaps because girls become responsive to language at an earlier age. Mothers start by carrying and sitting with both sons and daughters facing them, but they turn the boys to face away from them at an earlier age than is true for the girls. Fathers, too, behave differently toward sons and toward daughters. In fact, paternal behavior may be even more discriminative than that of mothers. Fathers have been found to give more than twice as many positive responses to their sons' behavior as to that of their daughters, while mothers gave the same number to both sexes (Margolin and Patterson, 1975).

The early years of life are a crucial period when a child must learn to identify correctly whether he is a boy or a girl. The child does this partly through learning about the physical differences between males and females, partly by observing adults' reactions to "girllike" or "boylike" behavior, and partly by observing how adult males and females act. By the time the child is three, he has learned a great deal about male and female behavior and has usually established a rather solid sex-role identity. No matter what happens in the future, it is unlikely that the sex role established by age three can be changed.

Why would anyone want to change an established sex role? It happens, rarely, that a child's sex is incorrectly identified at birth. Genetic anomalies, or the effects of certain drugs taken by the mother during pregnancy, may cause a clitoris to grow to the size appropriate for a penis, or the penis to remain the size of a clitoris. When the error of sex assignment is later discovered, surgery can make the person's anatomy fit his chromosomal sex. If the child has already been reared for some years as a member of the opposite sex, psychological sex reassignment is much more difficult. When a person has learned to act like a male, it is almost impossible to learn to act like a female instead.

Psychological sex reassignment is much easier if the child is still very young—under eighteen months or so of age. One dramatic case of psychological and physical sex reassignment involved twin boys, seven months old. The penis of one was completely destroyed in a circumcision accident. When the children were seventeen months old, sex reassignment of the injured boy was advised. The child was given a girl's name, dressed in girl's clothing, and treated as a girl. Relatives and the other children were informed that a mistake had been made and that the child was a girl. As a result of being treated as a girl, the former boy was described some years later in these terms (Money and Ehrhardt, 1972, 121-122):

"She likes for me to wipe her face. She doesn't like to be dirty, and yet my son is quite different. I can't wash his face for anything. . . . She seems to be daintier. Maybe it's because I encourage it." Elsewhere in this same recorded interview, the mother said: "One thing that really amazes me is that she is so feminine. I've never seen a little girl so neat and tidy as she can be when she wants to be. . . . She is very proud of herself, when she puts on a new dress, or I set her hair. She just loves to have her hair set; she could sit under the drier all day long to have her hair set. She just loves it."

The influence of the father in the first three to five years of life is crucial in establishing desirable personality characteristics in both boys and girls. The identification of a boy with the male role is encouraged if his father is both masculine in behavior and nurturant toward his child. The more the father cares for the baby and plays with him, the stronger the attachment the baby develops. However, if the father is present but weak and passive, masculine identification in the son is deterred. "Father-present boys with ineffectual fathers are not more masculine (and may even be less masculine) than father-absent boys" (Biller, 1971, p. 34). When the father is absent, the mother's attitude determines the boy's sex-role identification. If she approves of masculine behavior and encourages it, her son is more likely to identify himself as a male than if she disparages and discourages masculinity.

Absence of a boy's father early in life commonly is reflected in later scholastic underachievement. When the father's absence begins before the son is two, the son is likely to be even less industrious and also more distrustful than if absence does not begin until age three to five. In girls, absence of the father early in life often produces no obvious problems until puberty, when the girl's relationships with males are disturbed.

Boys in the United States experience more emphasis on establishment of a sex role than girls do. Little girls have more behavioral alternatives than little boys; girls may wear dresses or pants, short hair or long, and play with dolls or trucks. Any choice receives reasonable approval from adults, at least until shortly before puberty. Boys, on the other hand, receive consistent pressure toward gender conformity. They are aware as early as age three of the sex typing of toys and activities. Girls up to the age of five or ten remain variable in their choice of things to do (Kagan, 1964).

Concern with the sex-role identification of little boys is reflected in the recent establishment of a number of therapy centers which specialize in teaching masculine walking, talking, and playing styles to elementary-school boys. (Although girls are subject to similar pressures, in the form of ballet schools and deportment classes, the stress is usually postponed until they are older.) The kinds of "nonmasculine" behaviors which bring little boys into therapy include these: (1) feminine dressing, (2) wearing lipstick or makeup, (3) preference for girl playmates, (4) a stated desire to be female, (5) feminine gesturing, (6) doll playing, and (7) aversion to boy's games (Zuger and Taylor, 1969). In attempting to change these behaviors, stress may be placed on increased association with men and on the boy's understanding of the male role in reproduction.

Morality

An essential part of socialization is development of a *moral code*. Social functioning is smoothed when people share expectations about the right way to behave. But it is not enough for people to have a set of rules about right and wrong things to do. New situations can always arise. A set of moral principles is needed to allow a person to make decisions and to understand that if stealing cupcakes is wrong, stealing peanut butter cookies cannot be right.

Moral maturity must go beyond conformity to rules. "The barbarities of the socially conforming members of the Nazi and Stalinist systems and the hollow lives apparent in our own affluent society have made it painfully evident that adjustment to the group is no substitute for moral maturity" (Kohlberg, 1964, p. 383).

But where does moral conformity derive from? Many parents and teachers would be happy to see conformity, even if no moral maturity were present. None of the traditional sources of moral training seems to be effective. Sunday school and Scouting are not related to the child's honesty. There is "no positive or consistent relationship between earliness and amount of parental demands or training in good habits—obedience, caring for property, performing chores, neatness, or avoidance of cheating—and measures of children's obedience, responsibility, and honesty" (Kohlberg, p. 388).

Instead, the child who conforms to a moral code is likely to be one who has been disciplined for misbehavior by the consistent application of *love-oriented punishment.* Love-oriented punishment does not involve physical force. Instead, there is a stress on loss of love or approval and social isolation as a consequence of bad behavior. Love-oriented disciplinary techniques seem to excel in the development of appropriate guilt and of moral principles.

A child with strong moral standards is also likely to have high *ego strength* or capacity to deal with and predict the environment. Kohlberg has listed these characteristics of the person with strong moral character: (1) high general intelligence; (2) the tendency to anticipate future events and to choose a greater remote reward over a lesser immediate reward; (3) the ability to focus attention; (4) the ability to control socially disapproved fantasies (for example, aggression); and (5) high self-esteem.

Children do not simply learn morality. Like their perceptual and cognitive abilities, their moral capacities improve with maturation. It is almost impossible to teach a child to think at a higher moral level than the one which is natural to his stage of development.

Moral judgment may be one aspect of cognitive development; a child's ability to apply moral principles may depend on his ability to think and solve problems. Piaget, the great theorist of cognitive development, has described a number of characteristics of moral development (Kohlberg, 1964).

1. When young children make moral judgments, they pay attention to the misdemeanor itself rather than to the intent of the perpetrator. When older, they consider what the miscreant wanted to do as well as what he succeeded in doing. Young children feel that a child who accidentally breaks twelve cups while trying to help his mother should be punished more severely than a child who breaks one cup on purpose.

2. A young child considers any act to be totally right or totally wrong. Situational ethics does not appeal to the young mind. It is much easier for a child to learn that something is completely forbidden than that it may be done under some circum-

stances. The child also assumes that everyone in the world would agree with his moral judgment.

3. A young child defines an act as good or bad depending on whether the actor is punished.

4. Young children find it very difficult to make moral decisions by imagining being put in another's place.

5. Children think that natural or accidental misfortunes occur to punish them for things they have done wrong.

These characteristics of childish moral thought are at odds with everything the "liberal" or "permissive" parent tries to teach, and may be distressing to parents who are trying to present an advanced view of morality to their children. Nevertheless, in spite of

Figure 13.
Age trends for use of the six stages of moral development. (From *Developmental Psychology Today*, p. 311. Copyright © 1971 by CRM Books, a division of Random House, Inc.)

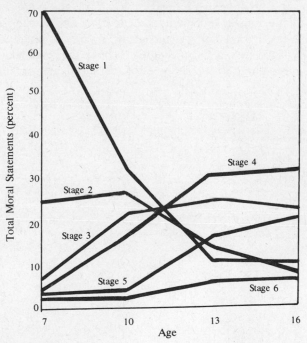

parental pressures, these primitive moral views persist for a time because of the natural course of the child's development.

Kohlberg has suggested that moral development involves a series of changing reasons for obedience to rules. (1) The child obeys in order to avoid being punished. (2) Obedience occurs in order to receive rewards. (3) The child conforms so that other people will like him. (4) Conformity is motivated by the desire to avoid the disapproval of the authorities, to maintain law and order. (5) Conformity to rules occurs as a result of a social contract concept. The person realizes he must give up certain satisfactions, as must all other members of the community, in order to bring about maximum community welfare. (6) Finally, Kohlberg feels, people develop to a moral stage where they do not feel required to conform to conventional rules or laws when convention is in conflict with some universal principle like the preservation of life.

Morality progresses through these stages in order, but it is hard to say at what age an individual will reach any stage. Teenagers sometimes make judgments at the level of the sixth stage, but Kohlberg found some college students who were still operating at the level of the second stage. Figure 13 shows the proportions of children using each of the six types of moral judgment at different ages.

Chapter 6
The Growing Mind

Long before he learns to talk, a baby begins to imitate the sound patterns of adult speech. It is crucial for him to hear the spoken language in order to learn to talk. His ability to discriminate sounds develops slowly, and his capacity for making certain sounds is even slower in maturing. The young child has his own ways of understanding the world, which are quite different from those of adults. A good environment will help stimulate intellectual growth and make it easier for the child to learn to read.

The growth of a child's intelligence is fascinating but mysterious to parents. Development goes on gradually, hidden beneath the surface, and is seen only in an occasional flash, when the child asks a new kind of question or solves a problem for the first time. But if you know what to look for, you can see many more events in the development of intellect than parents usually notice. In this chapter we will note the stages of development which can be seen in the child's understanding of space and of numbers; in the growth of language, in thinking, and in reading skills.

Intelligence Tests and the Infant

First, perhaps we should point out that intelligence testing cannot predict how bright a young baby will be when he grows up. There are tests of intelligence for children between birth and two years of age, but they are useful primarily for telling whether a child is normal or unusually slow. The older a child becomes, the better intelligence testing can predict his school performance and adult abilities. There is little correlation between a child's tested intelligence at three, six, or nine months and at five years, but tested intelligence at two years is much more closely related to test results at five years of age. There are probably two reasons for this.

First, tests for infants and for children probably test different abilities. Second, the child's experience and his environment strongly affect his intelligence, and they do so in ways which begin to be apparent by the age of two and which are even more evident by five.

Language Development

The development of language begins at birth. Newborn babies respond differently to adult speech than they do to other sounds. During the first year of life, babies change the sounds they make so they conform more and more closely to the language they hear their parents speak. Early in his life, the infant makes a wide variety of sounds—all the vowels and consonants known to human tongues are produced by the baby, even though his parents find it impossible to make some of the sounds themselves. Try sitting with a six-week-old baby in your lap and imitating some of the sounds he makes as he looks intently at your face; you will find that some of his noises are impossible for you to imitate, although they may well be found in some language you do not speak.

But as the first year of life progresses, a baby's parents find that they can imitate more and more of his noises. The baby is changing his sound productions so they are more and more like the sounds his parents make. For instance, the proportion (not the absolute number) of "d" sounds he produces comes to match the proportion of "d" sounds in the language he hears spoken. This change occurs long before the infant utters an intelligible word,

Figure 14.
The order of articulation of English phonemes. Stars indicate that 75 percent of children can pronounce the given phoneme; dots indicate that 95 percent can pronounce it. (After *Developmental Psychology Today,* p. 169. Copyright © CRM Books, a division of Random House, Inc.)

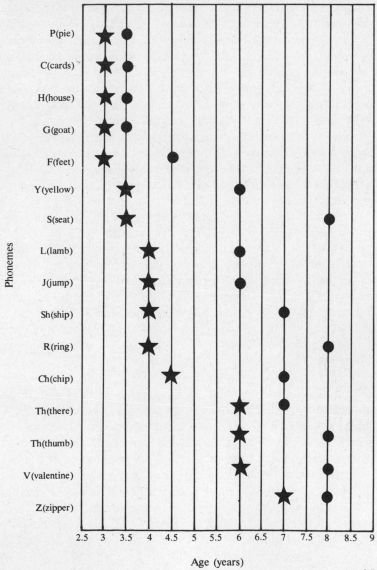

and in fact has begun long before he shows a sign of understanding any words. By the time the child is twelve or fifteen months old, the sounds he makes are like "English spoken in the next room"— they have all the sound characteristics and rhythms of his parents' language, though the listener may find no meaning in them at all.

The "moral" of these facts about language development is clear. In order for the baby to change his noises to resemble those made by his parents, and therefore for him to become capable of imitating his parents' pronunciation of actual words, *he must hear plenty of speech.* It does not matter whether the speech consists of spontaneous words or material which is read aloud. It does not even matter whether the adult uses real words or baby talk, because baby talk in any language uses the same kinds of sounds and rhythms as the adult form of the language. But the child must hear the language which will be his, in order to make a lot of sounds which are characteristic of that language, and to stop making sounds which adult speakers of the language never use.

Even though the child learns early to use the sound patterns of the language he is learning, it may be years before he can voluntarily produce all the sounds needed in that language. Children tend to follow a consistent order of learning to pronounce sounds, in English or whatever other language they first learn. For instance, at age three, seventy-five percent of children can pronounce the sound "p" (as in pie), but it is not until the age of seven that seventy-five percent can pronounce "z" (as in zipper). Figure 14 shows what proportions of children can pronounce particular sounds at different ages.

Of course, the child has to learn to *hear* differences in sounds as well as to pronounce them. Hearing differences is a stumbling block for adults learning foreign languages; they feel they are saying exactly what their teacher says, but they continue to make errors because they literally cannot tell the difference. The same problem occurs with young children. They might respond appropriately to what they think has been said, but in fact they confuse different words because they cannot tell certain sounds apart. Table 12 shows the order in which sound distinctions become meaningful for children. As the table shows, if a child cannot tell the difference between "which is *cool*?" and "which is the *tool*?"

Table 12
Emergence of discriminations
between speech sounds (10 to 23 months of age)

Order	Ability	Examples
1	Distinction of /a/ from all other vowels	father
2	Discrimination of front from back vowels	she vs. shoe; red vs. road
3	Discrimination of higher vowels from middle vowels	bead vs. bed; book vs. boat
4	Can tell when a consonant* is present	bed vs. ed; dish vs. ish
5	Distinction of nasals and stops	meat vs. beat; no vs. go
6	Distinction of nasal and "liquid" sounds	mess vs. less; new vs. you
7	Distinction between nasals	map vs. nap
8	Nasals and liquids distinguished from sibilants	moo vs. zoo
9	Lip and tongue consonants distinguished	big vs. dig; bun vs. gun; fox vs. socks
10	Stops and spirants distinguished	pull vs. full; do vs. zoo
11	Front and back of the tongue distinguished	done vs. gun; tight vs. kite
12	Voiced and voiceless consonants distinguished	pig vs. big; sue vs. zoo; few vs. view
13	Hissing vs. hushing distinct	seat vs. sheet
14	Distinction of liquids from y	yes vs. less

*Initial consonants are regularly distinguished before final ones, so a child hears the difference between map and nap before he can hear the difference between came and cane.

(From *Developmental Psychology Today*, p. 168. Copyright © 1971 by CRM Books, a division of Random House, Inc.)

there is no point in telling him "eat the *meat*, not the *beets*," or "sit on the *seat*, not on the *sheet*." If you know that a child cannot make a distinction at, say, level 3 in the table you will almost always be right in thinking that he cannot distinguish differences at level 4 or 5 or anywhere lower down. In order to cut down the number of arguments and misunderstandings between adults and young children, adults would do well to be aware of these facts and try not to use words which a child may not be able to tell apart from other words. (The child, of course, is unaware of his lack of comprehension. One fourteen-month-old, told that he was a tease, smiled gaily and pointed at his few teeth.) Learning to tell the differences between sounds also depends on whether the sounds come at the beginning or at the end of a word. Consonants at the beginning of a word are discriminated earlier than the same consonants at the end of words; the child can tell "meat" from "beat" before he can tell "mom" from "mob."

Of course, the ability to hear sound differences develops long before the ability to pronounce sounds correctly. A child wants people to talk to him using the pronunciation he can hear as correct, not the one he uses himself, and he gets very annoyed if an adult answers his question about "wabbits" by talking about "wabbits" instead of "rabbits."

Learning to Use the Language

Although children distinguish sounds at the beginnings of words earlier than the same sounds at the end of words, they have a tendency to listen to the ends of sentences rather than the beginnings. Perhaps it takes them so long to start to pay attention to what is being said that they simply miss the first words. In any case, this tendency gives rise to many a quarrel between parents and toddlers, and is the real reason why one should not use many negatives with one- and two-year-olds. A typical case of this misunderstanding arises when a parent says "Don't wipe your hands on your shirt!" The child hears "Wipe your hands on your shirt" and obediently does so, leading to annoyance for the parent and confusion for the child. This problem can be avoided by saying "Wipe your hands on the towel," or "Eric, please don't wipe your hands on your shirt."

The three- or four-year-old may pay attention mostly to the beginnings and ends of sentences, while the middle slips past him. Thus an explanation like "The dog doesn't go in the road because he doesn't want to get run over" may receive the bewildered reply "Why does he want to get run over?"

Children's understanding of grammar is often less advanced

than adults think. Three-year-olds are very poor at understanding passive constructions. If you tell them, "The boy was chased by the lion," they will often conclude that the boy was chasing the beast. They may find it difficult to remember whether a pronoun is nominative or accusative, a problem which is shown when a three-year-old says, "Her went to the store."

At three or four, the child may seem to begin making certain grammatical errors when he has previously used the words or constructions correctly. He may say "it broke" when he is two years old and "it breaked" when he is three. Correcting these "mistakes" is pointless as long as the child regularly hears people use the correct form. In fact, making errors like these is evidence that the child is advancing in his understanding of language. The two-year-old who says "it broke" uses the correct form because he has learned it by rote as an individual expression. When at age three he says "it breaked," he is showing a new comprehension that language has rules for forming past tenses, plurals, and so on. He has not yet learned that some verbs are irregular, so he forms the past tense of "break" according to the normal rules he has figured out in his three years of listening to people talking. He is not yet ready to deal with exceptions to the rules, and no amount of criticism or prompting will make him ready.

Thinking and Understanding

As far as the newborn baby can tell, the world has no rules. People can appear and disappear; mother can be in two, three, or four places at once, depending on the number of mirrors on her dressing table; even the baby's own body is unknown territory, from which a pink or brown object ending in five chubby projections may float up to the baby's field of vision. The baby has to learn that objects still exist when he cannot see them, that they are the same objects when he sees them from new angles and distances. He has to learn that objects do not really get smaller as they move farther away—they only appear to do so. A major task for the young infant is to learn that sizes, shapes, and so on, only appear to change with angle and distance, and that the world really possesses reliability and *constancy*. Even the three- or four-year-old may not have the adult's complete understanding of size and distance. This can be seen in children's comments when looking down from a high building—"why are the cars tiny, mommy?"—or when landing in an airplane—"everything's biggest again!"

Some fears and concerns shown by children can be traced to this lack of understanding of the physical world. Many one- and two-year-olds will be afraid of the bathtub or the toilet because they think they can go down the drain. They cannot yet accurately compare the sizes of their bodies and of drains and conclude that they are too big to go down. This kind of understanding cannot be taught or forced. It must come as part of the child's natural intellectual development.

Young children can similarly be distressed and confused by adults' casual or even careful explanations of the world. One three-year-old, told that babies grow in their mothers' tummies, was upset for several days before he asked whether women ate babies. This seemed to him a perfectly logical conclusion, since eating was the only way he knew of getting things into tummies.

There are a number of important ways of thinking which children learn in the first seven or eight years of their lives. Within these styles of thought, children's minds work rather differently than those of adults. This fact may lead to arguments between parent and child and to behavior which adults cannot predict or understand.

One concept which children must acquire is that of *object permanence*. This is the idea that there can be only one of a particular object or person; that it can be in only one place at a time; that it cannot move from one place to another without traveling through space; and that it still exists even if it cannot be seen.

Many three-month-olds seem startled if they see their mothers in a mirror as well as directly. They have begun to learn that there is only one mother; but they still have to learn that she can be expected to go on existing and to return after she goes away. When they do not see mother, they seem to feel that there is no mother anywhere. Older babies are fascinated by objects which go away and come back again, as you can see when they watch a jack-in-the-box or play peekaboo with vast amusement. By the time a baby starts to like peekaboo, he has gotten the idea that the vanishing person may still exist, but he does not have much faith in this belief and is greatly relieved on each occasion to see the person come back. Younger babies—say, at three or four months of age—will usually just become bored and look away when mother "vanishes" behind a blanket. Their attitude seems to be that she's gone and they had better find something else interesting to look at.

You can easily tell when a child has a highly developed sense of object permanence. Show him a small object which interests him; then, before his eyes, hide it under a scarf or a diaper. A baby who has little idea of object permanence will simply look around and then interest himself in something else. A baby who knows that the object still exists will lift the scarf and find the object. Object permanence development does not stop there, though. Other tests, increasing in difficulty, will show later stages of development. Older babies will be able to solve one or more of these problems:

1. An object held in the hand is moved under one scarf, moved out again and shown to the baby, moved under a second scarf, and finally left under a third scarf.

2. An object held in the hand is moved under two scarves and left under a third, but concealed in the hand between scarves.

3. An object is placed in a box and then dumped out under one scarf in a series; the box is then placed where the child can reach it.

A child may be two or three years old before he can find the hidden object immediately in all these situations. In other words, it may take several years of growth and development before a child's understanding of the physical world begins to resemble an adult's.

Babies have to develop patterns of thinking as well as of perception of the world. There are many ways of thinking, apparently easy for adults, which are simply impossible for babies and young children. For instance, many children under three years of age cannot understand that things look different to people who are standing in different places. A mother of a toddler may find that when she points at an object between herself and the child, the child does not turn toward her so he can see the object, but instead turns away from her to look in the direction her hand is pointing. He is imitating her, not understanding that the world looks different from where his mother is standing. He is *egocentric;* he thinks the world is just as he sees it and is the same for everyone. He is the center of his universe.

To tell whether a child can understand that other people see things differently, a simple test can be done using a card with a picture of a cat on one side and a picture of a dog on the other. Let the child examine it, then hold it up between you and ask, "What do you see?" and "What do I see?" If he answers that you see the same thing, he is still egocentric. If he answers correctly, he has at least begun to understand the difference in points of view.

The child who is strongly egocentric shows this characteristic in his speech. He may announce, "He went in his room and took his boat away from him," without letting his listener know whether one or four "hes" are involved. When misunderstood or questioned, the child at this stage may become furious and is obviously convinced that the adult is only being stubborn, since the meaning of the statement is clear to anybody (in other words, to the child himself).

The preschool child does not have the ability of *conservation.* This means that he thinks that trivial changes in an object can change important qualities like number or weight. Children generally acquire the ability to conserve number first of all, at age six or seven. This means that when they see ten pennies lined up, they know that ten pennies will still be there whether they are spread over twelve inches or pushed together into six inches of space. The preschool child, who cannot conserve number, thinks that the spread-out line has more pennies and the pushed-together line has fewer. He also thinks that changing the shape of a piece of clay changes the amount and weight of the clay. He believes that you can cover different amounts of a table with blocks if you arrange the same blocks differently. When water is poured from a tall, thin glass into a short, wide one, the preschool child thinks the amount of water becomes less. Perhaps this has something to do with the preschooler's tendency to pour too much into a glass; he thinks the pitcher and the glass contain the same amount, even though it is clear to an adult that they do not.

Learning to Read

In our literacy-oriented society, a crucial stage in the development of a child's mind is the period when he learns to read. He must read in order to be a full citizen of the Western world. People who cannot read find themselves unable to get a driver's license, to read a bus's destination, to follow written directions in cooking or on a medicine bottle, to obtain all but the most menial jobs. Thus parents quite understandably hover over their children, anxious to see whether the little ones will learn to read easily and well and show themselves capable of success, or whether they will be failures in life by the age of eight or nine.

An increasing concern with "perceptual handicaps" has made some parents overly sensitive to errors made by their preschool children. Things which indicate real reading problems when done by seven-year-olds do not necessarily, or even usually, mean reading problems when three- or four-year-olds do them. One mother became exceedingly concerned and labeled her child "dyslexic" when, at the age of three, he persisted in confusing "b" and "d." This kind of confusion is almost universal among three-year-olds and should not have upset the mother, had she known how most three-year-olds act. (In fact, her worries made the child very suspicious about learning to read when he was old enough to do so; he already expected to fail.)

Reading is not just one simple skill. It can be broken down into a whole series of subskills. What are the tasks which a child must be able to master before he can learn to read?

1. He has to be able to tell straight lines and curved lines apart (for instance, I versus S).

2. He has to be able to tell the difference between pointed figures (like A or V) and straight or curved lines.

3. He has to be able to tell open from closed figures (O versus C).

4. He has to be able to tell the difference between right and left (b versus d).

5. He has to be able to tell top from bottom (b versus p).

Before we discuss the ages at which children can usually perform these tasks, let me remark that we could eliminate a lot of unnecessary heartache by using *only* capital letters with children up to the age of eight or so. The capital letters of our alphabet offer fewer chances for confusion than do the lowercase letters. Using lowercase letters, children have the problem of discriminating b, d, p, and q; the problem vanishes when they are presented with B,

D, P, and Q instead. Lowercase t and f are confusingly alike—T and F are much more strikingly different. M and N are easier to discriminate than m and n. Since books are especially printed for school children, it would be quite easy to confine their type to capital letters. The only rationale for using lowercase letters seems to be that small children should write small letters.

The ability to tell right from left is not strongly developed in most children until at least the age of six. Earlier than that, a child may be able to tell you what objects are on his left or his right side, but he becomes very confused when you turn him around so the sides are reversed. Nine-year-olds can do nearly perfectly on naming left and right, but many people show some improvement even after the age of nine. The point is that a perfectly normal child between the ages of six and nine may sometimes or often confuse mirror-image letters like p and q and that this may not indicate any long-term perceptual handicap whatsoever.

Young children do not seem to be very concerned about whether things are right side up or upside down. They do not feel disturbed about looking at upside-down picture books, the way adults do. Eighteen-month-olds are frequently seen bending over with head on the floor, regarding the upside-down world between their legs.

Nonetheless, the evidence seems to be that preschool children recognize shapes best when they are right side up—in their normal orientation. One of their problems in learning to read may be that they do not know they can recognize letters better if they put the book or paper in a particular position. Even though small children will happily look at letters in almost any position, they do not "see" the tilted or upside-down letters as well as adults do. Three- or four-year-olds have trouble recognizing tilted pictures, while five- to seven-year-olds do much better.

Children below the age of 6 are often not interested in where the top or bottom of a letter ought to be. This leads to confusion of p and b and of q and d. Between the ages of six and eight, most children change their preference for orientation to agree with that of adults and begin to pay attention to a letter's vertical orientation.

To give you an idea of the frequency of letter confusions in

Table 13
Frequencies of letter confusions in young children

	d-b	d-p	d-q	b-p	b-q	q-p	q-b	q-d	b-d
Kindergarten	93%	50%	35%	40%	42%	96%	43%	27%	87%
First grade	65%	19%	13%	19%	15%	62%	11%	13%	60%

(Adapted from I. P. Howard and W. B. Templeton, *Human Spatial Orientation,* 1966, p. 346. Used by permission of John Wiley and Sons, Inc.)

young school children, Table 13 shows the percentages of children confusing d, b, p, and q.

As you can see, very large numbers of the kindergartners made right-left confusions.

Of course, I do not mean to suggest that no preschool child can learn the alphabet and the rudiments of reading. Given a child who is interested and adults who cooperate, it is frequently possible for very young children to learn to recognize and name the capital letters. A common time for children to be interested is about eighteen to twenty-four months of age, when many children are building up vocabulary and ask all day long, "What's that? What's that?"

However, many perfectly normal children may get to be eight or nine before their perceptual abilities have matured enough for them consistently to avoid b, d, p, and q confusions. We probably ask many children to start learning to read much too young—and the curse of the lowercase letters makes matters even worse for them.

What Is a Good Environment?

This chapter, so far, seems to suggest that maturation is more important than education in the development of a child's mind. This is true to a certain extent, for it is difficult to teach irregular verbs to a child who has just learned about the regularities of language, or conservation to a child who is just developing object permanence. But it is also true that some environments produce quicker and brighter children than others.

Children tend to grow up to be able to do the things their parents like to do. If you like to read and do it a lot, chances are that your child will like to read and be good at it. If you like to talk to your child and have him talk to you, chances are that his language development will be quick. But if you don't like to read and don't like to talk, your attempts to encourage your child in those directions "because he ought to" are likely to fail. The home where people talk, read, and are interested in intellectual problems is the home which is most likely to produce an intellectually oriented child.

Especially when their children are very young, parents often ask themselves, "How much stimulation is enough?" How much do you need to talk to the child? How much reading to him is enough? How many books and how many toys are enough to make a rich environment? These questions are hard to answer in specific terms, but there is a test you can apply to your home in order to decide whether your child is being stimulated appropriately. The original scale, Caldwell's "Inventory of Home Stimulation," has seventy-two questions, but it can be summarized in this way (Yahraes, 1968). A child's development is fostered by these home circumstances:

    1. A relatively high frequency of adult contact involving a relatively small number of adults (the mother, the father, and, when the mother is away, one of not more than three regular substitutes).

    2. The provision of a social learning environment that both stimulates the child and responds to him. (For example, the mother reads to the child at least three times a week, responds to him verbally when he vocalizes, tells him the names of things and people, encourages developmental advances such as waving bye-bye and saying his name, and supplies toys that challenge him to develop new skills. She gives these toys added value in his eyes by demonstrating her own interest in them.)

    3. An optimal level of need gratification, defined as sufficiently prompt attention to the child's needs so that the young organism is not overwhelmed, but not so prompt or complete that budding attempts to meet his needs himself are aborted or extinguished.

    4. A positive emotional climate—an interpersonal situation through which the child learns to trust others and himself. (For example, . . . the mother spontaneously praises the child's qualities or behavior, does not shout at him or express annoyance with him [when seen by an outside observer], caresses him at least once, and reports that no more than one instance of physical punishment occurred during the preceding week.)

5. An environment that contains few unnecessary restrictions on the child's early exploratory attempts. (The child is kept in playpen or jump chair no more than an hour a day, is taken promptly from his crib when he awakens from a nap, is not slapped or spanked for spilling or spitting food or drink.)

6. The provisions of rich and varied cultural experiences. (. . . whether or not the child eats at least one meal a day with his parents, is taken into a grocery store at least once a week, goes on an outing with his family at least every other week, is taken to church by a member of the family twice a month or more.)

7. A physical environment containing modulated amounts and varieties of sensory experience. (For instance, the house is not overly noisy and is neither dark nor monotonously decorated, and the family has at least one pet, one houseplant, and ten books.)

8. Access to certain kinds of play materials. For a child under one year, these include a cuddly toy; items like beads and blocks, that go in and out of a receptacle; a push or pull toy; a fit-together toy; and one or two cloth or cardboard books. For a child between one and two years of age they include a child-size table and chair; a ride toy such as a scooter or kiddy car; large blocks or boards, bang and hammer toys; access to a record player and to children's records. For a child between two and three years of age, they include simple wooden or heavy rubber puzzles; medium-sized wheel toys; role-playing toys, such as those used in playing at being a cowboy or a mother; and at least twenty children's books.

According to Dr. Caldwell's work, homes which score high on these factors tend to produce children whose tested intelligence increases over time, while the low-scoring homes tend to produce children whose scores on intelligence tests decrease. In any case, the parents who can see that their home rates high on Caldwell's inventory can feel content that they are doing what they need to do to support their children's intellectual development.

Chapter 7
Physical Growth and Abilities

Children grow and develop at the head end of the body before the legs and feet mature. Practice helps in the development of physical skills, but maturation must have taken place before practice can be effective. Changes in bodily proportions during the preschool years help in the development of physical skills. These skills are important for early social success. The perceptual and motor skills needed in drawing develop slowly and are important precursors of the ability to read and write. Though this perceptual motor development is crucial, perceptual-motor training programs do not appear to be effective in helping children with learning disabilities. The growth of play depends partly on physical skills, but also involves social and cognitive development.

The newborn baby "just lies there." The one-year-old crawls rapidly and walks a few tottering steps. The five-year-old tricycles, draws rocketships, does jigsaw puzzles, and picks up the cat in spite of its determination to stay on the floor.

In an earlier chapter we discussed the programs of physical development between birth and one year of age. The present chapter will be concerned with the physical growth, the neural de-

velopment, and the postural changes which accompany the child's
progress from toddler to kindergartner.

Principles of Development

The *cephalocaudal* principle, mentioned earlier, still applies
for the age range one to five. The capacities of the upper parts of
the body develop before those of the lower torso and limbs. It has
also been suggested that a *proximal-distal* principle operates: muscles closer to the midline of the body come under control before
those which are farther away. Large muscle movements, too, are

Table 14
The development of creeping

1   One knee and thigh forward beside the body
2   Knee and thigh forward, inner side of foot contacting the floor
3   Pivoting
4   Inferior low-creep position
5   Low-creep position
6   Crawling
7   High-creep position
8   Retrogression
9   Rocking
10 Creep-crawling
11 Creeping on hands and knees
12 Creeping, near step with one foot
13 Creeping, step with one foot
14 Quadruped progression (creeping on hands and feet).

Note: This is a good example of cephalocaudal development. The baby uses his
arms for prone progression until step 11, when the legs come into the picture for
the first time as effective instruments in forward motion.
(From *A Child's World: Infancy Through Adolescence* by D. Papalia and S. Olds,
p. 154. Copyright © 1975. Used by permission of McGraw-Hill Book Company.)

said to develop before *fine* motor control takes place. Table 14
shows how creeping develops according to these principles.

Maturation versus Learning

Obviously, some skills must be learned. A child who has
never seen a tricycle does not know how to tricycle. But many
abilities shown by young children are present largely as a result of
maturation. Training will not help such abilities appear significantly earlier than they would in the natural course of development. Walking, climbing, and jumping are good examples of
abilities which depend largely on maturation.

Some societies put severe restrictions on the activity of infants and toddlers. Some American Indian tribes tied infants to cradleboards for most of the day, in order to make carrying easier and so the babies could be hung up high, away from the cooking fire and the dogs. In a number of societies, notably pre-Revolutionary Russia, infants were swaddled in tight bandages between birth and a year or so of age. In traditional Bali, babies were carried until they were able to walk; they were never allowed to crawl because that was "animallike."

Nevertheless, in all these societies, motor development was unaffected by these restricting practices. Within a few days of the child's release from the cradleboard or swaddling clothes, he crawled, sat up, or even began to walk. The maturation of the nervous system had been going on at a normal rate in spite of the lack of practice or exercise.

When a preschooler is unable to do a good job of catching a ball or standing on one foot, making him practice does not usually help. Further maturation is needed before the task can be carried out. Sometimes the child cannot even conceptualize the task yet, so that he insists he is really skipping, for instance, when adults can see that he is running. When he cannot understand what the task means, there is little benefit to be derived from coaching.

Shape, Growth, Posture, and Motor Skills

Between the ages of one and five, a child's height increases considerably. Being taller is in itself helpful for the improvement of motor skills. The taller child can reach higher, climb better, and jump farther, just because he is bigger and stronger.

Changes in proportions also occur in the course of preschool growth. The arms and legs grow quickly, while the head does not make up as much of the child's height as it once did. (The two-year-old's head makes up about one-fourth of his total height, while the five-year-old's head accounts for only about one-sixth of his height.) A "quick and dirty" test of child development, used in some primitive societies to measure whether a child has reached "school age," involves a comparison of limb and head size. The child is asked to reach *over* the top of his head with his right hand and to touch his left ear. The proportions of a five-year-old make this possible, while a two-year-old cannot do it.

With longer arms and legs and broader shoulders the body has mechanical advantages which improve motor skills tremendously. Consider which would hit harder: a ball tied to a one-foot string and whirled around, or a ball tied to a three-foot string. The length of the arm makes a similar difference to the strength of a throw or a blow, just as the length of the leg makes a difference to the strength of a kick.

The child's balance may also improve when the head no longer makes up such a large proportion of his body. The center of gravity is lowered as the torso and limbs become relatively long, so falling over becomes less likely. (Though boys are a bit heavier than girls during this stage, the girls have longer arms and legs, which help account for their better physical control and lesser proneness to accident.)

There are considerable postural differences between one-year-olds and five-year-olds. The younger children tend to be pot-bellied and swaybacked, and to stand with feet wide apart and knees slightly bent. With maturation, the back straightens, the feet come closer together, and the child becomes capable of walking with the knees straight.

Hand and Eye Preference

As a child matures, he develops a preference for the use of his left or his right hand. This preference is determined to some extent by training but it depends primarily on the development of the brain. As the cortex matures, a balance is reached so that either the left or the right cortical half dominates the other. Since the left side of the cortex has control over the motor functions of the right half of the body, while the right cortex controls the left side, a *right-handed* person has a dominant *left cortex.*

Dominance of the left side of the cortex (right-handedness) is most common among human beings. Heredity seems to play an important part in determining which side of the cortex will dominate. However, cortical dominance and hand preference are not established at birth. Hand preference fluctuates through early life and finally settles down in middle childhood. "Often hand preference seen in infants . . . will tend to 'blur' as he reaches the age of two and begins to focus his attention on his feet, which seem to need all the visual monitoring they can get in order to properly perform their locomotive function" (Cratty, 1970, p. 128). Preference for the use of the right or the left eye is determined in the same way as hand preference. "Mixed" or "cross" dominance occurs when a person prefers the left hand, but the right eye, or vice versa. It was once thought that mixed dominance caused problems of thinking or perception, but this is probably not the case. Among normal children, about fifty percent have mixed dominance.

Balance

The maintenance of balance requires a pattern of complex activities governed by different parts of the body. Simple upright standing involves a constant monitoring of muscle tensions by the nervous system. When one muscle becomes fatigued, the whole pattern of muscle tensions must be adjusted, or the person will fall over. This is accomplished through unconscious reflexes and would be far too complicated to do voluntarily. Balance also takes into account messages from the inner ear, which indicate the position of the head relative to the pull of gravity, and the tension of the neck muscles, which shows where the head is relative to the body. Cues from vision are also taken into account, so that balancing with eyes closed is more difficult than with eyes open.

Children under two years of age have enough trouble walking normally or on a wide balance beam. They cannot do much in the way of more complicated balancing. After three, however, the ability to balance improves. A three-year-old can usually stand on one foot briefly. Girls seem to progress more quickly than boys in the development of balance skills. Table 15 shows the ages at which particular skills are likely to appear.

Walking, Running, Hopping, and Skipping

Toddlers have to watch their feet and look where they are going constantly when they *walk*. As a result, walking is an activity which is relatively hard to combine with anything else. Unfortunately, the manufacturers of pull toys do not seem to understand this. An eighteen-month or two-year-old finds it very hard to walk along pulling a toy and glance over his shoulder at it from time to time. Walking is hard enough without turning, finding an object

Table 15
Motor activities in early childhood

Approximate Time of Appearance	Selected Behaviors
1 year	Walking unaided
	A rapid "running-like" walk Will step off low objects
2 years	Walking rhythm stabilizes and becomes even Jumps crudely with two-foot take-off Will throw small ball 4-5 ft
	True running appears
	Can walk sideward and backward
3 years	Can walk a line, heel to toe, 10 ft long
	Can hop from two to three steps, on preferred foot Will walk balance beam for short distances Can throw a ball about 10 ft
4 years	Running with good form, leg-arm coordination apparent, can walk a line around periphery of a circle
	Skillful jumping is apparent
	Can walk balance beam
5 years	Can broad-jump from 2-3 ft Can hop 50 ft in about 11 seconds Can balance on one foot for 4-6 seconds Can catch large playground ball bounced to him

(Reprinted with permission of Macmillan Publishing Co., Inc. from *Perceptual and Motor Development in Infants and Children* by B. Cratty, p. 61. Copyright © 1970 by Bryant J. Cratty.)

visually, turning back, and, once again, figuring out where he is. Some toddlers try to walk backwards so they can look at the toy, but they are not very good at glancing around to see where they are going. A much more appropriate toy for the one who must look when he walks is a *push* toy, like a toy lawn mower or vacuum cleaner.

A true *run* involves a stage where both feet are off the ground simultaneously. A toddler's "run" does not include this stage. Instead, it is a quick walk in which the child lifts a foot, falls forward slightly, and sticks out the foot to catch himself.

Hopping on one foot is more complicated than walking, but simpler than skipping or galloping. Most three-and-a-half-year-olds can hop one or more steps. By the time the child is five, he becomes able to hop eight or ten steps in a row. Girls show advanced development in hopping before boys do. When hopping is done rhythmically, as in some dances where two hops on the left foot alternate with two hops on the right, very few five-year-olds can carry out the pattern accurately.

Approximately 80 percent of five-year-olds are unable to *skip*. When they try, they usually skip with one foot and walk with the other. *Galloping,* too, is too difficult for most preschoolers.

Throwing and Catching

In his discussion of throwing, Cratty (1970) suggests that "[the] infant may find that a hand-held object is suddenly 'pulled away' from him as he rapidly swings his arm in a sudden movement. The sound the missile makes as, for example, it strikes a vase and the visual display and other effects that the object elicits will probably encourage him to make renewed voluntary attempts to duplicate the throwing action. His first attempts at throwing are usually a rigid underhand motion. During the second, third, and fourth years the child will usually evidence a wide variety of throwing patterns, as he will seem to be searching for efficient work methods in this type of complex motor task" (p. 54).

By the age of five or six, throwing skills are improved by the addition of two factors which are rarely seen in younger children. First, a weight shift from foot to foot is carried out as the child releases the ball, thus giving the ball greater velocity. Second, the child learns to take a step as he releases the ball.

Catching also goes through a series of levels of development. Children under three-and-a-half usually hold their arms straight out, with elbows stiff, ready for passive reception of a ball. At about the age of four, the elbows remain stiff but the hands are open. In one study, about 50 percent of five-and-a-half-year-olds were capable of the last stage of catching competence—holding arms and elbows against the sides of the body while waiting for the ball to arrive.

In one of Cratty's studies, it was found that by five years of age the average child could catch a ball (eight inches in diameter) three or four times out of five attempts when the ball was bounced from a distance of fifteen feet. Girls did better than boys on this task, though boys did slightly better (in another study) on bouncing a tennis ball once with both hands and catching it once with both hands.

Physical Development and Social Success

We often think of physical skills as crucial for the social success of high school boys—the football captain has plenty of friends, while the ninety-seven-pound weakling has none. In fact, this pattern of social acceptance for the physically skillful is also important for both boys and girls of preschool age. Physical maturity rather than a special personality determines friendships among young children. A number of studies (described by Cratty) have noted the high status children achieve by good physical performance. Physically accelerated boys are given positions of leadership because they are considered acceptable by adults and by other children. The status achieved through physical ability is greater for boys than for girls.

Though physical maturity helps bring about athletic proficiency, maturation alone cannot do the entire job. Practice is important in the development of special skills like catching and throwing. Thus it is important for a child to have access to athletic materials and places to use them from an early age, and it is equally important to have available an older person who can encourage and help the child work on his skills.

Body Image

Every person has some concept of the size and shape of his body. The existence of this body image is evident in the fact that we can estimate accurately whether we can walk through a small space or whether we can reach an object without bending forward. A child's body image differs from an adult's in a number of ways. First, it may be relatively vague because it takes a certain level of intellectual development to understand the relations between body parts. Second, lack of experience and difficulty in using a mirror leave a child relatively ignorant about his back, his buttocks, his ears, and the top of his head. And, third, the fact that the child is still growing necessitates a constant change in his body image.

Table 16 shows the basic stages in the development of body image. As you can see, the understanding of left and right is a crucial part of the body image development. It contributes, too, to the ability to perform a number of tasks: get shoes on the correct feet, discriminate between "d" and "b," set the table with knives and forks in the right places. Chapter 6 discusses the development of left-right discrimination in more detail.

Cratty has developed a scale which evaluates a child's body image development (see Table 16). Testing a child with this simple scale can give some insight into his understanding of his physical makeup.

Drawing

Drawing is a physical skill whose development is very important in our culture. It is a quiet activity which adults like children to perform. It leads to a better understanding of concepts of color, shape, and size. It exercises and develops fine control of the hands and fingers. Above all, it prepares the child for an interest in writing and thus in reading.

The attitude which a child below the age of three or four brings to drawing is very different from that of an adult. The young child is interested in *process,* not *product*—in the act of drawing, not the drawing as an object. He does not really care what his picture is "a picture of," although he understands that pictures can represent things and can identify them when they are realistic. He may know that a cow has two horns and start by drawing two, but then become so fascinated by the process of drawing horns that his cow ends up with fifteen of them. This is not a matter of inaccuracy, ignorance, or inability to control the crayon, but instead involves an emphasis on carrying out certain activities rather than on producing a picture for other people to look at.

The young child's drawing is also affected by the fact that he is *egocentric.* He cannot see things from other people's point of view, and he assumes that everything looks the same to other people as it does to him. He also has a great deal of faith in the

Table 16
Body image development

Age	Perceptions Formed
0-2 years	At the end of this period, the child can sometimes identify gross body parts verbally; can touch "tummy," back, arm, or leg when asked to do so, seems aware of toes before leg
2-3 years	Becomes aware of front, back, side, head, feet, and can locate objects relative to these body reference points; begins to gain awareness of more body parts, i.e., thumb, hand, feet, etc.; parts of face learned
4 years	Becomes aware that there are two sides of the body and knows their names, but not their location; more detailed awareness of body parts gained; can name little finger and first fingers
5 years	Knows that there is a left and right side of the body, but is usually confused concerning their location; can locate self relative to objects, and objects relative to self; trunk appears in figure drawings
6 years	Begins to distinguish left and right body parts and to locate body relative to the left and right of things and objects relative to the left and right of the body; becomes aware of little finger and ring finger and names them
7-8 years	Concept of laterality well established; begins to correctly distinguish the left and right of other people and name correctly their left and right movements; facial expressions appear in figure drawings; limbs are filled in and details appear in figure drawings
9-10 years	Adopts other individual's perspective with ease; can describe the arrangement of objects from another's point of view

(Reprinted with permission of Macmillan Publishing Co., Inc from *Perceptual and Motor Development in Infants and Children* by B. Cratty, p. 112–13. Copyright © 1970 by Bryant J. Cratty.)

knowledgeability of adults and believes that since they know everything they must know what he draws without his working on a realistic representation.

A common admonition to parents and nursery school teachers warns against asking a child what he is drawing. I myself have never understood the reasoning behind this. Even very young children know that pictures can represent real objects, and children of all ages are rather objective about the resemblance of their drawings to reality. They know that they do not always do things exactly right. Obviously one should not criticize or ridicule the drawing, or try to teach the child to be more representational unless he requests help. But, unless the child is annoyed by the intrusion, just asking seems harmless enough. "Tell me about your picture" is a good way to make this inquiry.

The general stages of development of drawing are the following:

1. Showing interest in pencils or pens, by holding them or making random marks on any handy surface (a wall, for instance. Fresh paint is preferred)

2. Crude scribbling. The child at this stage may bring the scribble to an adult and ask what he has drawn. He has no preconceived plan about what he is drawing, nor can he figure out what the drawing resembles once he has completed it.

A related point here is that the young child has not learned the conventions of Western representational drawing and so may not always recognize line drawings as adults do. For instance, two converging lines may be seen by an adult as a road going off in the distance, but the child may see the figure as a Christmas tree, an upside-down ice cream cone, or simply two converging lines. A foreshortened figure which the adult sees as a circle or square observed from an angle may be described by the child as "squashed." Thus, the child may feel that the adult has some special ability for labeling line drawings, which he himself is lacking.

3. Production of lines and squares, balanced out by scribbles.

4. Simple geometrical figures.

5. Combinations of figures and more accurate coloring of figures. "Elaborated designs" which are not clearly representational.

6. Representational drawings of houses and people.

Children's Drawings as Tests of Development

Children's drawings have been used as ways of assessing the

intellectual and the *emotional* development of their creators. Since children follow a fairly predictable path of development in their ability to draw, a set of drawings can make a good intelligence test. In fact, there are high correlations between level of drawing maturity and both tested intelligence and school performance. Using children's drawings as a test of their emotional status involves a major problem. Children's drawings are quite variable. Some days a child will produce very elaborate, advanced drawings; other days his work is very simple (see Figure 15). It has been suggested that any diagnosis based on drawings should deal with a whole series of drawings by the child, rather than just one or two.

Perceptual-Motor Therapy

Whether a child is developing normally or abnormally, chances are that his parents have been exposed to certain ideas on the use of directed movement as therapy for perceptual, motor, intellectual, and emotional difficulties. Many people with retarded or brain-damaged children have seized on motor therapy with tremendous hope. Even some parents of normal children have felt they could improve their children's behavior or help them mature faster by means of movement therapy.

Unfortunately, the major motor therapy programs do not seem to produce reliable improvement in children's skills. In addition some of them involve tremendous practical problems in application. It is also noteworthy that some such programs appear to contradict in their theories a great deal which research has found to be true about the central nervous system.

The two major perceptual-motor therapy programs which we will discuss here are those of Delacato and of Getman. The former stresses general patterns of motor development, while the emphasis of the latter is on visual movement skills.

The Delacato Program

Delacato's approach is based on the idea of retraining the functions and interrelations of parts of the brain by making the child retrace the milestones of motor development which normally occur in the first two years of life. He also advocates the development of strong dominance of one cerebral hemisphere by having the child use only one hand. An unusual additional factor

Figure 15.
A series of drawings by a three-and-a-half-year-old girl.

4/28/77

5/2/77

5/5/77

5/6/77

in Delacato's program is the exclusion of music from the child's experience, in accordance with the theory that the nondominant hemisphere is involved in listening to music and will have its influence unduly strengthened if music is heard.

The Delacato method is complex and time-consuming, involving as it does the deliberate movement of the child's limbs through prescribed patterns by adult helpers. The children involved often resent the program, since it forces them to do "babyish" things like crawling even though they consider themselves to be "big kids." In addition, careful research has provided almost no evidence that children improve on virtually any measure as a result of the Delacato program.

The Getman Program

Getman suggests that poor reading is caused by eye problems brought on by the stress of too early exposure to reading. His therapy for these problems emphasizes, among other things, training in visual tracking—the capacity of the eyes to follow a moving object without losing sight of it.

Other researchers in this area contend that difficulty in reading is rarely related to poor tracking. Instead, when ocular problems are present, they more usually involve difficulty in fusion of images of nearby objects—the capacity to combine the images from the two eyes into a single picture.

Again, there is little evidence supporting the effectiveness of Getman's program.

Other Suggestions

Cratty has pointed out that children with reading problems and other "perceptual-motor" difficulties have many individual differences. Different children may derive the most benefit from different therapy programs. Cratty suggests that "the child from the higher-income home may benefit more from increased exposure to motor activities than the child from the lower socio-economic areas. The latter may be improved more educationally by exposure to verbal-linguistic tasks and exercises rather than balance-beam walking" (p. 265).

Whatever the effect of Delacato's and Getman's programs on children with physical and intellectual problems, the programs ought *not* to be used on children whose functioning is within the normal range for their age. This is occasionally proposed by parents who feel they would like their children to be more advanced in performance, or that the children could do better if they were pressed in some way. Normal children are not likely to benefit from therapies whose use is questionable even for children with problems. In addition, the rigors of the therapeutic program are likely to engender resentment in the children and to create in them a quite unjustified sense of inadequacy. Parents who are tempted to use a therapeutic program where none is really needed should perhaps examine their motivations and inquire whether their concern is not with their own social status rather than with the child's welfare.

The Growth of Play

Whatever their physical skills, young children do a lot of quarreling when they play together. Three years of age is the worst period for this; the child is old enough to be persistent about what he wants, but too young to have the social skills to get his way without fighting. With increased age, social skills grow so that group play works better. These social skills may take the form of bossiness, especially in the case of preschool girls. Selfishness tends to diminish slowly as the child learns that other children do not like him to be demanding or refuse to share.

Preschool children feel a strong need for companions at their own level of maturity. They want to play with people, and adults are not really interested in the games preschoolers like. Because of their deep need for playmates, preschool children who do not have companions often develop imaginary playmates, especially between the ages of two-and-one-half and four-and-one-half, or may become very attached to a pet. Neither of these can be more than a temporary solution to the need for companionship, because they cannot respond to the child's affection or attack as a real human playmate would.

Boys learn earlier than girls that certain toys and forms of play are considered appropriate for their sex. By the age of four or five, children may begin to show a preference for their own sex as playmates. Girls do not care for the physical aggressiveness of boys, and the boys resent the bossiness common among girls of this age.

Younger children are more likely than older children to like to play with toys. Social play is less oriented around toys than play alone, and as the child feels an increased need for companionship he moves away from his earlier, more solitary toy play. Toy play, when carried out in groups, brings up the problem of sharing, which is hard for preschoolers and young elementary school children to handle by themselves. Thus the child may find he enjoys group play more in the absence of toys and the consequent fights over sharing.

Preschool children, especially bright ones, can learn to play card games and board games with surprising success, if they have sufficient adult supervision. They must be reminded frequently of the necessity for taking turns or performing the parts of the game in the prescribed order. There is relatively little competition or interest in "winning" at this age. Fascination with the process of playing far outweighs any interest in demonstrating personal superiority.

Preschool children find it quite hard to learn and remember a set of formal rules for a game. They blithely move their opponent's checker, or take a domino out of turn. In a few years, however, they not only learn the rules but also become very rigid about them. They are convinced that there is only one way to play a game, and that way cannot be modified to suit an extra player or a lost card. Only with the approach of adolescence does their inflexible thinking about rules begin to soften.

The Utility of Play

Play and physical activity are the work and the education of young children. Through their endless physical activity, children gain control over their bodies. Through dramatic play, they gain understanding of their own roles in life and of adult activities. Even the most apparently aimless play with toys involves intellectual growth. One four-year-old arranged toy cars in different sequences for an hour, then announced, "Mommy! Four and four and four make twelve!" He would never have held still long enough for an adult to teach him that item of arithmetic, but through play he achieved understanding by himself.

Chapter 8
Socializing the Child

Certain tricks, such as controlling the amount of eye contact, make it easier to control a child's behavior. The sentence structure used in talking to a child may be related to his obedience. Behavior modification uses reward and punishment to change behavior. Shaping is a behavior modification technique which is essential for bringing about new ways of behaving. Consistency is essential in the use of punishment, but matters are different when reward is used. The concept of "time out" helps prevent the accidental rewarding of undesirable behavior.

What Adults Want

No child is a social being when he is born. The newborn is (and should be) a completely selfish, totally biological being, whose only interests have to do with his physical survival and growth. He does not care about other people's needs or even know that they exist as feeling, thinking beings. Gradually, though, the biological dangers of early life pass. The baby's survival is prac-

125

tically assured. He himself can take time off from his concern with nursing and sleeping. He can look around him and begin to learn something about other people and his relationship with them.

When the baby has passed through the basic stages of early development, and particularly by the time he can walk, his culture sets out on the process of *socialization*. Every culture in the world employs its own techniques of teaching a child to act like the older people in his world: to use their language, to eat the way they do and to prefer the foods they like to eat, to use their customs of elimination, to practice modesty in dress and in speech—and, for that matter, to hate and fear the things the adults hate and fear.

Some techniques of socialization which parents use were learned during their own childhoods, as a result of watching their parents or other adults dealing with children. Even if a person objects to a child-rearing technique which is experienced at an early age, he has learned it thoroughly, and he may find himself using it inadvertently when under stress. (How many people who were slapped as children swear they will never slap their own offspring, but find themselves doing just that when there is a problem in the middle of the night?) If the person approves of the methods he learned early, he may never even question whether or not they are the best ways of socialization.

Many parents in the United States today are in the peculiar position of having been isolated from any early experiences of child rearing. When a person comes from a small family, chances are that all of the children were fairly well socialized before the oldest was ready to start school. Chances are, also, that the parents took all the responsibility for child rearing and never assigned such responsibilities to the oldest child. In school, the children were age-graded and did not experience many interactions with children younger than themselves.

As a result, people need to be taught techniques for socialization. This is one of the reasons for the immense expansion of interest in behavior modification. Parents and teachers seek guidance on how to socialize their children, and researchers have tried to respond to this need.

This chapter will deal with some general concepts and hints for dealing with children and with the theory and practice of behavior modification whereas Chapter 5 discusses the major socialization problem for young children: toilet training.

General Hints for Dealing with Children

The person who gets along well with children usually has a variety of tricks which smooth the way and encourage cooperation. Sometimes these tricks are so subtle that the beginning parent or teacher cannot even see what is happening—it just looks as though the successful adult has "a way with children." However, it is possible to analyze at least some of the tricks and teach them to adults who do not have that "way" with children. Here is some advice given to parents and teachers by a successful cooperative day-care center (The Treehouse Preschool, Pinehurst, New Jersey).

How can we be most effective in dealing with the children? Some special ideas are outlined below, but one concept should govern all interactions with the children. *Any time you interfere with children's behavior, you should have the goal of changing the behavior*—changing it to more desirable behavior which will last a long time, rather than just temporarily stopping some activity. Never approach a child with the goal of punishing him, "teaching him a lesson," or "giving him what he deserves."

Such approaches can be very satisfying for the angry adult, but they can make the child's behavior worse in the long run.

Now, how do you go about changing a child's behavior? Here are some ideas: some practical rules to follow, and some attitudes which lead to effective work with children.

• Don't give a child a direct order unless you can—and intend to—enforce it. Undesirable behavior is encouraged when parents tell a child what to do, but allow him to disobey or show that they are powerless to cope with him.

Example: Don't tell a child directly to eat his sandwich or to stop crying. You are not capable of making him do these things. Suggestions or comments may work: "I think you'll be hungry later if you don't eat your lunch." "I know you're unhappy, but I can't help you unless you stop crying and tell me what's wrong."

• Try to avoid using too many negatives.

Example: "Don't play with the blocks now; don't scream; don't hit Susie" will soon wear out your patience as well as the child's. Suggest alternatives: "How about playing with the trucks, since the blocks are put away?" Say "please" when you must forbid an activity.

• Sometimes children listen only to the last part of what you say. The result is that they obediently do just what they were told not to do. This is another reason to phrase things positively.

Example: "Don't wipe your hands on your shirt" may result in a dirty shirt. "Wipe your hands on a towel" works better.

• There are two kinds of physical *force* which may be useful.

(a) A child in a wild tantrum may be held tightly around the body (hugged against you) until his rage is spent. This would be appropriate only for a child who is really out of control.

(b) When a child is being uncooperative, it helps to tell him to look at you while you talk. If he refuses, gently but firmly turn his chin toward you and hold it until you finish what you have to say. This works well when a child pretends not to hear you.

• Deal with children at their own physical level. Kneel or sit on the floor.

• Learn to find out what the child considers the problem to be. It may be more or less serious in his opinion than in yours.

Example: A two-and-one-half-year-old hit a four-year-old over the head with a piece of cardboard. The four-year-old became enraged and also seemed frightened. When questioned, she communicated her belief that any blow could break her head, and she looked at her hand fearfully after touching her head, apparently expecting to see "insides." When assured that her head could not be broken by being hit with toys or paper, she quickly calmed down and went back to playing. (The younger child was reminded that hitting hurts people and makes them angry.)

Example: A three-year-old seemed fascinated by an empty shampoo bottle and half-fearfully told a baby-sitter that it was "yucky." The sitter told him it was not, but he insisted and repeated his remark several times. A parent who was listening guessed that the child's mother must have told him shampoo was yucky in order to keep him from drinking it. She remarked that shampoo was yucky to drink, but was good to wash hair with, and that it was okay to play with the bottle. The child agreed and went off to play again. (The sitter should have guessed from the child's insistence that he was especially concerned about what he was saying.)

• If a child bites someone, pinching his nostrils gently together cuts off his air supply and persuades him to let go. Don't bite him back!

• Children need to learn acceptable ways of expressing anger. A time when you've just stopped a child from hitting or

biting is ideal for this. Here are some possible things to encourage:
(a) verbalizing feelings, using the words "angry" or "mad"
(b) yelling loudly (outdoors if necessary)
(c) building up blocks and knocking them down
(d) throwing things at a target (not a living one!)
(e) for older children, drawing angry pictures or making up
angry stories
   • Always follow up discipline with comfort, explanation,
and discussion. Don't leave the child confused and unhappy,
even if you are annoyed with him. Help him talk about his feelings of fear, anger, and sadness. If he cries or shouts at you, tell
him what you think he is feeling. This helps distract him from
the original problem and also helps him learn to understand
and control emotions. Try to understand his ways of describing
his feelings. A small child may tell you that something "bothers
his tummy" rather than that it frightens him.
   • When a child is frightened, shy, or dependent, never ridicule him or call him a baby. Try to find out the reason for his
fears.
   • There is rarely any need to make critical comments when a
child has a toilet accident. You should be prepared to be comforting while you change his clothes, since he may well be sob-
bing bitterly in his distress over his loss of control.
   • If a child is playing constructively and happily by himself,
don't interfere. Don't offer to show him how to build with
blocks or to draw, unless he asks you to. You can sit down on
the floor by him if you want to make yourself available to him.
   • Some children (but not all) will drop an obstinate pose
quickly if you tell them to come to eat, put on their jackets, etc.
when they are ready rather than "right now." They are often
ready at once when there is no direct order to fight about.

   A few additional comments may be added to these. The use of
eye contact, for instance, is very important in dealing with children. When you look a young child straight in the eye, his response is very like that of a dog or cat: he feels threatened and/or
dominated by you. (Next time a dog barks at you, try an experiment. Look him in the eye for a while and see how the barking and
growling continues; then drop your gaze and see how quickly he
loses interest in you.)
   There are three important ways in which eye contact can be
used with children. First, when you are dealing with a child who is
frightened or unfamiliar with you, you should avoid much eye

contact. Adults are sometimes so concerned with the child that they are constantly gazing at him. This sustained eye contact can be very distressing for the child. Instead, glance at him briefly, then avert your gaze; then glance at him again, and so on. When he seems to be warming up a bit, then you can look into his eyes for a longer period.

When you are on good terms with a child, you probably use eye contact in a second way. Even a child under a year of age will seek eye contact as a way of sharing pleasure or interest. The baby who is watching romping kittens and laughing will frequently turn to look at his mother or father and share the fun through eye contact. Such sharing is a good way to strengthen the bond between parent and child.

Eye contact can also be used in a third way: to quell rebellion and exact obedience. When you look a child in the eye as you speak to him, it becomes much harder for him to refuse to do as you say. Children recognize this and try to turn their faces away when told to do something they would rather not do. Sometimes they seem to think that eye contact will make their parents do as they are told, too, and shout "*Look* at me, mommy! *Look* at me!" when refused a lollipop or new toy.

Behavior Modification

Behavior modification is a method which changes a child's behavior by reward, and sometimes by punishment. It is based on three principles: (1) that when a behavior is followed by reward, it begins to occur more frequently; (2) that when a behavior is never rewarded, it becomes less frequent; and (3) that punishment can stop undesirable behavior at least temporarily.

The modification of behavior through reward and punishment has become one of the great fetishes and one of the great bugaboos of child rearing in our time. There seem to be two major points of contention involved: first, whether it is morally right to use rewards to get children to behave as desired, and, second, whether such techniques actually work.

People who oppose behavior modification on moral grounds usually seem to feel that children *ought* to be good, that they *ought* to be punished for misbehavior, and that rewarding them for good behavior is bribery. This is all very well, except that centuries of punishment of criminals have shown that punishment alone does very little to change behavior from bad to good, and research in learning theory (which we will discuss below) shows that reward *is* effective in changing behavior. There is no getting around the fact that when a child behaves well, he, his parents, his teachers, and his friends all are happier, work better, and like each other more than when he behaves badly. Thus, good behavior is worth working for, from everyone's point of view. Why, then, abandon a method which can make life more pleasant for everyone, on the grounds that, morally speaking, bad behavior should be punished and good behavior ignored?

Behavior modification techniques certainly do work, *if they are applied correctly.* Like any other techniques, they may or may not work if applied in a slipshod fashion. Here are some important things to understand about behavior modification.

Punishment Punishment alone is not very effective, because it tends to arouse so much emotion in the child that he forgets why he is being punished. However, when punishment for an undesired behavior is combined with reward for a desired behavior, learning may be even faster than when reward alone is used. For instance, you want the child to use a hanky rather than wipe his nose on his sleeve. Punishment for wiping on the sleeve will not work very well unless you also reward for using the hanky, but punishing one and rewarding the other will work better than rewarding for using the hanky alone.

Punishment also presents the problem that the behavior may start up again as soon as the punishment is discontinued. For instance, in one study (Kauffman and Scranton, 1974) the parents of a two-year, nine-month-old girl wanted to use behavior modification to stop their daughter's thumb-sucking. During regular sessions of reading aloud, the mother would stop reading every time the little girl put her thumb in her mouth. The girl stopped sucking her thumb during reading time, but not at other times—and began again as soon as the punishment was discontinued. When the parents used praise and material rewards for refraining from thumb-sucking for stated periods of time, however, the sucking diminished, and remained diminished, both at reading time and at other times.

Timing To be effective, either reward or punishment must

come as soon as possible after the behavior you want to modify. Whatever behavior occurs just before the reward or punishment is the behavior which will be modified. So, if you say "Just wait until your father gets home! He'll spank you for writing on the wall," you are arranging a punishment which will have almost no effect on the behavior which concerns you—writing on the wall. Similarly, if a child shows good table manners and you want to reward him so he will be more likely to be mannerly in the future, you must do so while he is still at the table. It is nice, but ineffective, to wait until you are at the store 2 hours later and present him with an ice cream cone as a reward for having good manners at lunch.

Being specific   In order to change the child's behavior effectively, you must know just what behavior you want. Reward and punishment cannot be used effectively to bring about vague general changes. It is no use saying, "I want him to speak more politely" or "I want better table manners." To change behavior effectively, the desired behavior must be defined specifically and in detail. For instance, we could define "speaking more politely" in these ways:

Saying "please" when making a request
Saying "May I?" rather than "Can I?"
Speaking only when no one else is speaking
Speaking quietly (that is, at the same loudness as adults)

And we could define "better table manners" in these ways:

Wiping face with napkin
Using knife and fork rather than fingers
Keeping mouth closed while chewing
Keeping elbows off table

Behavior modification can be used effectively only when a desired behavior can be broken down into well-defined units.

Shaping   It is easy to reward a behavior when it occurs occasionally. Matters become much more difficult when the behavior is rarely or never seen. How do you reward a child for dressing himself—and thus make it more likely that he will do so in the future—if he breaks out into tears and refusals and complaints when he has one sock halfway on? The answer is that the reward should not be saved for the moment when the child has completely dressed himself, buttoned all his buttons, and tied his shoes. Instead, at the beginning, a reward should be given for anything which involves a *part* of the dressing activity. Then, over a period of days, more and more dressing should be required before the reward is given. This process is called *shaping*. For instance, the following program might be followed:

Days 1–2: Reward for sock half on

Days 3–4: Reward only for sock all the way on

Days 5–6: Reward only for both socks on and so on

When the task is very difficult or the child very resistant, it may be necessary to use more sessions or to divide the task into

Table 17

Conditioning successive approximations of pill-taking behavior

Day	Session Number (10-20 Trials Per Session)	Reinforced Behavior
1	1-5	No success in eliciting acceptance of pill.
2	1-2	Touch cheek with forefinger.
	3-4	Touch lip with forefinger.
	5	Touch cheek with forefinger; pill between thumb and middle finger.
3	1	Same as last session.
	2-3	Touch lip with forefinger; pill between thumb and middle finger.
	4	Touch cheek with pill approximately 1 in. from corner of mouth.
	5	Touch cheek with pill approximately ½ in. from corner of mouth.
4	1	Touch corner of mouth with pill.
	2	Touch lips in center of mouth with pill.
	3-4	Touch teeth with pill.
	5	Place pill behind teeth; touch tongue with pill.
5	1	Same as last session.
	2-5	Stick tongue out; touch tongue with pill.

(From L. Wright, J. M. Woodcock, and R. Scott, "Conditioning Children when Refusal of Oral Medication Is Life-Threatening," *Pediatrics,* 1969, *44,* 959-972. Reprinted with permission from the American Academy of Pediatrics.)

still smaller steps. For instance, Table 17 shows a reward program used with an eighteen-month-old girl who was suffering from leukemia and who desperately resisted taking medication by mouth. She was rewarded by a piece of candy, a hug, and praise for cooperating.

Shaping is probably the most misunderstood aspect of behavior modification—and it is one of the most essential for effective use of this technique. One of my students was recently working as a volunteer in a center for handicapped preschoolers, where behavior modification was a primary training technique. He was assigned to work with a four-year-old girl who never talked. The plan was that he should show her pictures in a book, and reward her whenever she named the picture—but only when she spoke the proper word aloud. After several frustrating weeks without a single word or reward, he came to ask for help. Once he understood the shaping technique, he began to reward her just for opening her mouth, then for forming the word with her lips, and finally for speaking audibly. Only a few hours of shaping were needed before the little girl began to talk spontaneously.

Reward   Food is commonly used as a reward in behavior modification. The best reward to use can be established only by experiment. An adult might learn quickly when rewarded by lobster Newburg rather than by lollipops, while a child's preferences might reverse the reward value of the two foods. Something which is liked but rarely had is a more effective reward than something which is experienced every day. In a serious behavior modification program, the food which is used as a reward should not be given except in the reward situation. Probably the most common food reward for children is M&M candy, with raisins running a close second.

Motivation   In order for a reward to be effective, the child must really want it. So, if you want a food reward to work, the child must be hungry—or, at least, hungry for the reward you are using. In serious treatment programs with disturbed children, the child may be deprived of *all* food except what he earns as a reward for the desired behavior. Most parents or teachers do not want or need to go this far, but they do need to make sure that the child does not get all he wants of the reward too quickly. So, one M&M or one raisin at a time should be used—not a handful.

Using praise as a reward   Praise, hugs, and kisses often work very well as a reward, because the child never gets "full" of them or tired of them. But, of course, a young child who does not understand language very well may do much better with M&Ms. Some children can be switched from candy to praise as a reward if you give the praise first, then the candy, for a while, and then stop giving the candy. (Candy first and then praise will not work.)

Preferred activity as a reward (the Premack principle)   One way to get a child to do things he does not like is to reward him by letting him do things he frequently does spontaneously. For instance, if he often runs around and around when no one tells him not to, a chance to run around and around will be an effective reward for a disliked activity (for instance, sitting still all through supper).

When you reward or nonreward inconsistently   Punishing an undesirable behavior may not be necessary, but rewarding it is obviously undesirable. The behavior is not going to stop if it is rewarded. Nevertheless, a reward for an unwanted behavior is sometimes given accidentally. Suppose you have decided that you will not reward a child who cries and calls after bedtime; you will not go to him, and eventually the unrewarded behavior will come to a halt. But one night you accidentally leave some necessary item in the child's room and you have to go in and get it when he is crying and calling. His misbehavior is thus unintentionally rewarded. And the unfortunate aspect is this: when a behavior is rewarded only occasionally, it will go on much longer than if it had been rewarded every time. This sounds wrong, but research has demonstrated its accuracy repeatedly. Thus, when you are trying to get rid of a behavior by nonreward, you should try to plan very carefully so that no accidental reward occurs. And, similarly, when you want to keep a behavior going, do not reward it every time after the shaping stage has passed.

This principle is especially important in cases where a child whines or fusses to get something. When the parent sometimes gives in after protracted fussing, the child learns that fussing for a long time is the thing to do. But he doesn't know *how* long to keep fussing, so his whining may go on longer and longer every time. It is sometimes very hard to grit your teeth and not give in, but the consequences of letting the child learn that continued whining gets rewarded are so unpleasant as to make gritting your teeth worthwhile.

(Punishment does not seem to work in the same way. Consistency of punishment is crucial if it is to be effective. But when you are manipulating rewards, forget about being consistent; it is actually inconsistency that does the trick.)

Time out: nonreward   One effective way to deal with undesirable behavior is to make sure that it is never rewarded. Unfortunately, this may be easier to say than to do. Ordinarily we think of rewarding a child as some specific, overt, positive act, but in fact there are many times when adults reward children without intending to do so.

For instance, suppose a child is frightened or lonely at night and calls his mother frequently. She gets tired of the constant calling and stamps into the bedroom to scold or even spank the youngster. Now, from the mother's point of view, what she has done is punishment. From the child's viewpoint, however, a reward may have been given—since the presence of an angry mother may be more satisfactory than no mother at all. In the same way, a child who wants attention may be rewarded by a look of annoyance from an adult.

Genuine nonreward is most likely to occur if the child is isolated temporarily after he does something undesirable. A "time out" from reinforcement is created by putting him in his room or sitting him in a special chair for a while, in order to keep social rewards from taking place. (And remember that social reward does not come solely from adults. The reactions of other children can reward and maintain behavior, too.)

With some kinds of behavior, the use of "time out" or nonreward does not work well. Some behaviors contain within themselves basic and intrinsic rewards. To take an extreme example, you could not stop a child from eating by withholding reward, because when one is hungry eating is a rewarding act in and of itself. Thus, scratching an itch or urinating when the bladder is full are not likely to be affected by *withholding* approval—though these behaviors may be changed to performance at different times or in different places when special rewards are *given*.

Alternative behaviors   Children are always doing something.

They rarely just sit, and most people would agree that just sitting is not a very desirable thing for a healthy child to do. Since children are active, one way to get rid of undesirable activities is to reward alternative things to do. In fact, if you can find an acceptable activity which is *incompatible* with the unacceptable one (that is, they cannot be carried on simultaneously), rewarding the acceptable behavior will gradually get rid of the undesirable one. A child cannot use a handkerchief and pick his nose with his fingers at the same time, so increasing his use of the handkerchief will automatically decrease nose picking. Looking for alternative behaviors can be a very fruitful approach to behavior change.

Modifying the environment   Behavior is partly based on the objects available in the environment. You cannot type without a typewriter, and a child cannot draw on the wall if he is lacking either a wall or a crayon. Sometimes the quickest and best way to get rid of problem behavior is to modify the environment. This is especially true with babies and young children. A ten-month-old can learn not to knock over the vase of flowers on the coffee table—but is it worth the effort of teaching him, when the vase can be left on the mantle for another year, after which a sentence or two of instruction can do the trick?

Some Important Criticisms
of Behavior Modification

As many critics of behavior modification have recently pointed out, even the expert cannot always figure out what rewards are causing some behaviors to occur. Some research has found that parents pay about equal amounts of attention to desirable and undesirable kinds of behavior, so we are not necessarily talking about a very simple situation where the reward is attention alone. Some parents and children may be so angry at each other that nothing done by either is rewarding to the other.

Reward can also function to remove the intrinsic satisfaction of carrying out a task. When rewards are used in certain ways, the child learns to do things in order to get the reward, rather than in order to feel proud and competent. As soon as the reward stops, the behavior stops. Naturally, this is undesirable, and critics of behavior modification have condemned the method because of this possible effect. One does not want to have to give a child an M&M every time he makes his bed until he is twenty-one years old. However, attention to some of the principles we discussed above can solve this problem. You should always use the smallest reward possible to maintain the behavior, and give it as infrequently as possible (only experimentation can tell you how small and how infrequent it can be in any individual case). Once shaping of the behavior is finished and it is being performed the way the adult wishes, it is time to reduce the amount and/or frequency of reward. You can start by rewarding every other time, then every third time, and so on. If you keep on this way, you will find that you can stop rewarding completely after a while, and the desirable behavior will continue.

In fact, this variation of reward is what happens naturally in many situations. The mother praises her toddler when he gets to the toilet on time because she is thrilled and relieved. After a number of successes, she gets used to the idea and forgets to praise him every time—and gradually praise becomes less and less frequent, until it disappears altogether. Nevertheless, going to the toilet remains a very reliable behavior which can go on for a lifetime without ever being praised again.

Supplementary Reading

Readers who are interested in more information on certain topics may want to look up the following references in the bibliography. The books and articles noted here are among the most useful sources I encountered while writing each chapter.

Chapter 1: The Newborn

Gaensbauer and Emde, 1973
Kron, Stein, and Goddard, 1966
Naeye et al., 1971
Rosenblith, 1974

Chapter 2: A Year of Changes

Foss, 1970
Simpkins and Raikes, 1972

Chapter 3: Children Have Temperaments

Chess, Thomas, and Birch, 1965
Toman, 1969

Chapter 4: The Developing Personality

Aisenberg et al., 1973
Bakwin, 1948
Bowlby, 1953
Caldwell, 1964
Gesell and Ilg, 1943

Chapter 5: Social Growth

Blehar, 1974
Bugental and Love, 1975
Foxx and Azrin, 1973
Green and Beall, 1962
Hoffman and Hoffman, 1964
Money and Ehrhardt, 1972

Chapter 6: The Growing Mind

Condon and Sander, 1974
Elkind, 1971
White, 1971
Yahraes, undated

Chapter 7: Physical Growth and Abilities

Cratty, 1970

Chapter 8: Socializing the Child

Wright, Woodcock, and Scott, 1969
Yawkey and Griffith, 1974

References

Ainsworth, M. D. S., and Wittig, B. A. Attachment and exploratory behavior of one-year-olds in a strange situation. In B. Foss, (ed.), *Determinants of infant behavior*. Vol. IV. London: Methuen, 1970.

Aisenberg, R. B.; Wolff, P. H.; Rosenthal, A.; and Nadas, A. S. Psychological impact of cardiac catheterization. *Pediatrics*, 1973, *51*, 1051-59.

Anders, T. F. The sleep of infants and children. *Sandorama*, 1975, *3*, 20-23.

Bakwin, H. Thumb and finger sucking in children. *Journal of Pediatrics*, 1948, *32*, 99-101.

Bakwin, H. Deviant gender-role behavior in children: Relation to homosexuality. *Pediatrics*, 1968, *41*, 620-29.

Barnes, C. M.; Kenny, F. M.; Call, T.; and Reinhart, J. B. Measurement in management of anxiety in children for open heart surgery. *Pediatrics*, 1972, *49*, 250-59.

Bayley, N. Individual patterns of development. *Child Development*, 1956, *27*, 45-74.

Becker, W. C. Consequences of different kinds of parental discipline. In M. L. Hoffman and L. W. Hoffman, (eds.), *Review of child development research*. Vol. I. New York: Russel Sage Foundation, 1964.

Bell, R. Q. Relations between behavior manifestations in the human neonate. *Child Development*, 1960, *31*, 436-77.

Bell, R. Q.; Weller, G. M.; and Waldrop, M. F. Newborn and preschooler: Organization of behavior and relations between periods. *Monographs of the Society for Research in Child Development*, 1971, *36*, 1-2.

Benjamin, L. S.; Serdahely, W.; and Geppert, T. V. Night training through parents' implicit use of operant conditioning. *Child Development*, 1971, *42*, 963-66.

Bernal, J., and Richards, M. P. The effects of bottle and breast feeding on infant development. *Journal of Psychosomatic Research,* 1970, *14* (3), 247-52.

Biller, H. B. Father absence and the personality development of the male child. *Developmental Psychology,* 1970, *2,* 181-201.

Biller, H. B. *Father, child, and sex role.* Lexington, Mass.: Heath Lexington Books, 1971.

Blehar, M. C. Anxious attachment and defensive reactions associated with day care. *Child Development,* 1974, *45,* 683.

Bostock, J., and Shackleton, M. G. Enuresis and toilet training. *Medical Journal of Australia,* 1951, *2,* 110-13.

Bothe, A., and Galston, R. The child's loss of consciousness: A psychiatric view of pediatric anesthesia. *Pediatrics,* 1972, *50,* 252-63.

Bowlby, J. Some pathological processes set in train by early mother-child separation. *Journal of Mental Science,* 1953, *99,* 265-72.

Bowlby, J. *Maternal care and mental health.* New York: Schocken, 1966.

Brazelton, T. B. Sucking in infancy. *Pediatrics,* 1956, *17,* 400-404.

Brazelton, T. B. A child-oriented approach to toilet training. *Pediatrics,* 1962, *29,* 121.

Brazelton, T. B. Crying in infancy. *Pediatrics,* 1962, *29,* 579-88.

Brown, R. M., and Brown, N. L. The increase and control of verbal signals in the bladder training of a seventeen month old child—A case study. *Journal of Child Psychology and Psychiatry,* 1974, *15,* 105.

Bugental, D. B., and Love, L. Nonassertive expression of parental approval and disapproval and its relationship to child disturbance. *Child Development,* 1975, *46,* 747-52.

Caffey, J. The whiplash-shaken infant syndrome. *Pediatrics,* 1974, *54,* 396-403.

Caldwell, B. M. The effects of infant care. In M. L. Hoffman and L. W. Hoffman (eds.), *Review of child development research.* Vol. I. New York: Russell Sage Foundation, 1964.

Caldwell, B. M. Can young children have a quality life in day care? In S. Coopersmith and R. Feldman (eds.), *The formative years.* San Francisco: Albion, 1974.

Carlsmith, L. Effect of early father absence on scholastic aptitude. *Harvard Educational Review,* 1963, *34,* 3-21.

Chess, S.; Thomas, A.; and Birch, H. G. *Your child is a person.* New York: Viking, 1965.

Condon, W. S., and Sander, L. W. Neonate movement is synchronized with adult speech: Interactional participation and language acquisition. *Science,* 1974, *183,* 99-101.

Coodin, F. J., Gabrielson, I. W., and Addiego, J. E. Formula fatality. *Pediatrics,* 1971, *47,* 438.

Coopersmith, S., and Feldman, R. (eds.). *The formative years.* San Francisco: Albion, 1974.

Cratty, B. J. *Perceptual and motor development in infants and children.* New York: Macmillan, 1970.

Curzon, M. E. J. Dental implications of thumb-sucking, *Pediatrics,* 1974, *54,* 196-200.

Developmental Psychology Today. Del Mar, Calif.: CRM Books, 1971.

Eckenhoff, J. E. Relationship of anesthesia to postoperative personality changes in children. *American Journal of Diseases of Children,* 1953, *86,* 587.

Egli, G. E.; Egli, N. S.; and Newton, M. The influence of the number of breast feedings on milk production. *Pediatrics,* 1961, *27,* 314-17.

Elkind, D. *A sympathetic understanding of the child: Birth to sixteen.* Boston: Allyn and Bacon, 1971.

Elmer, E. Failure to thrive: Role of mother. *Pediatrics,* 1960, *25,* 717-25.

Etaugh, C.; Collins, G.; and Gerson, A. Reinforcement of sex-typed behaviors of two-year-old children in a nursery school setting. *Developmental Psychology,* 1975, *11,* 255.

Etzel, B. C., and Gewirtz, L. D. Experimental modification of caretaker-maintained high-rate operant crying in a 6 and a 20 week old infant (Infans Tyrannotearus): Extinction of crying with reinforcement of eye contact and smiling. *Journal of Experimental Child Psychology,* 1967, *5,* 303-37.

Fagot, B. I. Sex differences in toddlers' behavior and parental reaction. *Developmental Psychology,* 1974, *10,* 554-58.

Fauls, L. E., and Smith, W. D. Sex-role learning of five-year-olds. *Journal of Genetic Psychology,* 1956, *89,* 105-17.

Flavell, J. H. *The developmental psychology of Jean Piaget.* New York: Wiley, 1966.

Forres, H. Emotional dangers to children in hospitals. *Mental Health* (London), 1953, *12,* 58-62.

Foss, B. (ed.). *Determinants of infant behavior.* Vols. I-IV. London: Methuen, 1970.

Foxx, R., and Azrin, N. Dry pants: A rapid method of toilet training children. *Behavior Research and Therapy,* 1973, *11,* 435-42.

Gaensbauer, T. J., and Emde, R. N. Wakefulness and feeding in human newborns, *Archives of General Psychiatry,* 1973, *28,* 894-97.

Gesell, A., and Ilg, F. L. *Infant and child in the culture of today.* New York: Harper, 1943.

Green, M., and Beall, P. Paternal deprivation—A disturbance in fathering. *Pediatrics;* 1962, *30,* 91-99.

Green, R., and Money, J. Effeminacy in pre-pubertal boys. *Pediatrics,* 1961, *27,* 286-99.

Greenberg, D. J.; Hillman, D.; and Grice, D. Infant and stranger variables related to stranger anxiety in the first year. *Developmental Psychology,* 1973, *9,* 207-12.

Greenwaldt, E.; Bates, T.; and Guthrie, D. The onset of sleeping through the night in infancy. *Pediatrics,* 1960, *26,* 667–68.

Gunther, M. Infant behavior at the breast. In B. Foss, (ed.), *Determinants of infant behavior.* Vol. IV. London: Methuen, 1970.

Guthrie, H. A. Effect of early feeding of solid foods on nutritive intake of infants. *Pediatrics,* 1966, *38,* 879–85.

Hart, B. M.; Allen, E. K.; Buel, J. S.; Harris, F. R.; and Wolf, M. M. Effects of social reinforcement on operant crying. *Journal of Experimental Child Psychology,* 1964, *1,* 145–53.

Heinstein, M. I. Behavioral correlates of breast-bottle regimes under varying parent-infant relationships. *Monographs of the Society for Research in Child Development,* 1963, *28,* No. 4.

Henderson, N. B., and Engel, R. Neonatal visual evoked potentials as predictors of psychoeducational tests at age seven. *Developmental Psychology,* 1974, *10,* 269–76.

Hoffman, M. L., and Hoffman, L. W. (eds.). *Review of child development research.* Vol. I. New York: Russell Sage Foundation, 1964.

Hoffman, M. L., and Saltzstein, H. D. Parent discipline and the child's moral development. *Journal of Personality and Social Psychology,* 1967, *5,* 45–57.

Howard, I. P., and Templeton, W. B. *Human spatial orientation.* New York: Wiley, 1966.

Howell, M. C. Effects of maternal employment on the child. *Pediatrics,* 1973, *52,* 327–43.

Hurlock, E. *Developmental psychology.* New York: McGraw-Hill, 1968.

Jackson, R. L.; Westerfeld, R.; Flynn, M. A.; Kimball, E. R.; and Lewis, R. B. Growth of "well-born" American infants fed human and cow's milk. *Pediatrics,* 1964, *34,* 642–52.

James, V. L., and Wheeler, W. E. The care-by-parent unit. *Pediatrics,* 1969, *43,* 488–94.

Johnson, M. M. Sex role learning in the nuclear family. *Child Development,* 1963, *34,* 319–33.

Johnston, C. M., and Deisher, R. W. Contemporary communal child rearing. *Pediatrics,* 1973, *52,* 319–26.

Kagan, J. Acquisition and significance of sex typing and sex role identity. In M. L. Hoffman and L. W. Hoffman (eds.), *Review of child development research.* Vol I. New York: Russell Sage Foundation, 1964.

Kauffman, J. M., and Scranton, R. R. Parent control of thumb-sucking in the home. *Child Study Journal,* 1974, *4,* 1.

Kearsley, R. B.; Zelazo, P. R.; Kagan, J.; and Hartmann, R. Separation protest in day-care and home-reared infants. *Pediatrics,* 1975, *55,* 171–75.

Kohlberg, L. Development of moral character and moral ideology. In M. L. Hoffman and L. W. Hoffman (eds.), *Review of child development research.* Vol. I. New York: Russell Sage Foundation, 1964.

Kopp, C. B. A comparison of stimuli effective in soothing distressed infants. *Dissertation Abstracts,* 1971, *31* (12-B), 7631.

Korner, A. F. Individual differences at birth: Implications for early experience and later developments. *American Journal of Orthopsychiatry,* 1971, *41,* 608–19.

Korner, A. F. Early stimulation and maternal care as related to infant capabilities and individual differences. *Early Child Development and Care,* 1973, *2,* 307–27.

Korner, A. F. Sex differences in newborns with special reference to differences in the organization of oral behavior. *Journal of Child Psychology and Psychiatry,* 1973, *14,* 19–29.

Kramer, P., and Hogan, K. A. Sex differences in verbal and play fantasy. *Development Psychology,* 1975, *11,* 145–54.

Kron, R. E.; Stein, M.; and Goddard, K. E. Newborn sucking behavior affected by obstetric sedation. *Pediatrics,* 1966, *37,* 1012–16.

Krusen, M. M. The relationship of physical condition at birth to intellectual functioning at early school age. *Dissertation Abstracts,* 1971, *32,* 2485.

Landreth, C. *Early childhood.* New York: Knopf, 1967.

La Voie, J. C. Type of punishment as a determinant of resistance to deviation. *Developmental Psychology,* 1974, *10,* 181–89.

Levin, F. M., and Fasnacht, G. Token rewards may lead to token learning. *American Psychologist,* 1974, 816–21.

Levin, S. Night cries in little girls. *Pediatrics,* 1969, *44,* 105.

Lewis, M. Infant intelligence tests: Their use and misuse. *Human Development,* 1974, *16,* 108–18.

Lewis, M., and McGurk, H. Evaluation of infant intelligence. *Science,* 1972, *178,* 1174–77.

Lewis, M. L., and Rosenblum, L. A. (eds.). *The effect of the infant on its caretaker.* New York: Wiley-Interscience, 1974.

Lillie, D. L. *Early childhood education.* Chicago: Science Research Associates, 1975.

Lobitz, W. C., and Johnson, S. M. Parental manipulation of the behavior of normal and deviant children. *Child Development,* 1975, *46,* 719–26.

Loda, F. A.; Glezen, W. P.; and Clyde, W. A. Respiratory disease in group day care. *Pediatrics,* 1972, *49,* 428–37.

Lombroso, C. T., and Lerman, P. Breathholding spells (cyanotic and pallid infantile syncope). *Pediatrics,* 1967, *39,* 563–81.

Maccoby, E., and Jacklin, C. Stress, activity, and proximity seeking: Sex differences in the year-old child. *Child Development,* 1973, *44,* 34–42.

Margolin, G., and Patterson, G. R. Differential consequences provided by mothers and fathers for their sons and daughters. *Developmental Psychology,* 1975, *11,* 537–38.

Marotsos, M. P. Children who get worse at understanding the passive.

Journal of Psycholinguistic Research, 1974, *3,* 65–74.

Marshall, S.; Marshall, H. H.; and Lyon, R. P. Enuresis: An analysis of various therapeutic approaches. *Pediatrics,* 1973, *52,* 813–17.

Mattson, A., and Weisberg, I. Behavioral reactions to minor illness in preschool children. *Pediatrics,* 1970, *46,* 604-10.

Maulsby, R. L. An illustration of emotionally invoked treta rhythm in infancy: Hedonic hypersynchrony. *EEG and Clinical Neurophysiology,* 1971, *31,* 157–65.

Menkes, M. M.; Rowe, J. S.; and Menkes, J. H. A 25-year follow-up study on the hyperkinetic child with minimal brain dysfunction. *Pediatrics,* 1967, *39,* 393–99.

Miller, R. N., and Fraumeni, J. F. Does breast-feeding increase the child's risk of breast cancer? *Pediatrics,* 1972, *49,* 645–46.

Miller, S. M. Effects of maternal employment on sex role perception, interests, and self-esteem in kindergarten girls. *Developmental Psychology,* 1975, *11,* 405–6.

Money, J., and Ehrhardt, A. *Man and woman, boy and girl.* Baltimore: Johns Hopkins, 1972.

Moss, H. A.; Robson, K. S.; and Pedersen, F. Determinants of maternal stimulation of infants and consequences of treatment for later reactions to strangers. *Developmental Psychology,* 1969, *1,* 239–46.

Mussen, P. H. (ed.). *Carmichael's manual of child psychology.* New York: Wiley, 1970.

Mussen, P. H.; Conger, J. J.; and Kagan, J. *Child development and personality.* New York: Harper and Row, 1969.

Naeye, R. L.; Burt, L. S.; Wright, D. L.; Blanc, W. A.; and Tatter, D. Neonatal mortality, the male disadvantages. *Pediatrics,* 1971, *48,* 902–6.

Olim, E. G. Maternal language styles and children's cognitive behavior. *Journal of Special Education,* 1970, *4,* 53–68.

Osofsky, J. D., and Danzger, B. Relationships between neonatal characteristics and mother-infant interaction. *Developmental Psychology,* 1974, *10,* 124–30.

Palmgrist, H. The effect of heartbeat sound stimulation on the weight development of newborn infants. *Child Development,* 1975, *46,* 292.

Paradise, E. B., and Curcio F. Relationship of cognitive and affective behavior to fear of strangers in male infants. *Developmental Psychology,* 1974, *10,* 476–83.

Pick, H. L. and Pick, A. D. Sensory and perceptual development. In P. H. Mussen (ed.), *Carmichael's manual of child psychology.* New York: Wiley, 1970.

Pontius, A. A. Neuro-ethics of "walking" in the newborn. *Perceptual and Motor Skills,* 1973, *37,* 235–45.

Rheingold, H. L. The effect of environmental stimulation upon social and exploratory behavior in the human infant. In B. Foss (ed.), *Determinants of infant behavior.* Vol. I. London: Methuen, 1970.

Riegel, K. F. Dialectic operations: The final period of cognitive development. *Human Development,* 1973, *16,* 346-70.

Roberts, K. E., and Schoellkopf, J. A. Eating, sleeping, and elimination practices of a group of two-and-one-half-year-old children. IV. Elimination practices: Bowel. *American Journal of Diseases of Children,* 1951, *82,* 137-43.

Roberts, K. E., and Schoellkopf, J. A. Eating, sleeping, and elimination practices of a group of two-and-one-half-year-old children. V. Elimination practices: Bladder. *American Journal of Diseases of Children,* 1951, *82,* 144-52.

Rosenberg, B. G., and Sutton-Smith, B. The measurement of masculinity and femininity in children. *Journal of Genetic Psychology,* 1964, *104,* 259-64.

Rosenblith, J. F. Relations between neonatal behaviors and those at eight months. *Developmental Psychology,* 1974, *10,* 779-92.

Rutter, M. Psychological development: Predictions from infancy. *Journal of Child Psychology and Psychiatry,* 1970, *11,* 49-62.

Sayer, D. J., and Allen, R. P. Factors influencing the suppressant effects of two stimulant drugs on the growth of hyperactive children. *Pediatrics,* 1973, *51,* 660-67.

Santrock, J. N. Relation of type and onset of father absence to cognitive development. In F. Rebelsky and L. Dorman (eds.), *Child development and behavior.* New York: Knopf, 1974.

Scarr, S., and Salapatek, P. Patterns of fear development during infancy. *Merrill Palmer Quarterly,* 1970, *16,* 53-90.

Schaffer, H. R., and Callender, W. M. Psychological effects of hospitalization in infancy. *Pediatrics,* 1959, *24,* 528-39.

Schwarz, J. C.; Strickland, R. G.; and Krolik, G. Infant day care: Behavioral effects at preschool age. *Developmental Psychology,* 1974, *10,* 502-6.

Sears, R. R.; Pintler, H.; and Sears, P. S. Effect of father separation on preschool children's doll play aggression. *Child Development,* 1946, *17,* 219, 243.

Serunian, S. A., and Broman, S. H. Relationship of Apgar scores and Baylay mental and motor scores. *Child Development,* 1975, *46,* 696-700.

Sidel, R. *Women and child care in China.* Baltimore: Penguin, 1973.

Simpkins, M. J., and Raikes, A. S. Problems resulting from the excessive use of baby-walkers and baby-bouncers. *Lancet,* 1972, *7753,* 747.

Smith, C. A. Pediatric practice: Human milk and breast-feeding. *Pediatrics,* 1964, *34,* 873-74.

Spelke, E.; Zelazo, P.; Kagan, J.; and Kotelchuk, M. Father interaction and separation protest. *Developmental Psychology,* 1973, *9,* 83-90.

Stayton, D. J.; Ainsworth, M. D. S.; and Main, M. B. Development of separation behavior in the first year of life. *Developmental Psychology,* 1973, *9,* 213-25.

Stayton, D. J.; Hogan, R.; and Ainsworth, M. D. S. Infant obedience and maternal behavior: The origins of socialization reconsidered. *Child Development,* 1971, *42,* 1057-69.

Stebbens, J. A., and Silver, D. L. Parental expectations in toilet training. *Pediatrics,* 1971, *48,* 451.

Stevens, J. A., and Silber, R. L. Parental expectations vs. outcome in toilet training. *Pediatrics,* 1974, *54,* 493-95.

Sutton-Smith, B.; Rosenberg, B. G.; and Landy, F. Father absence effects in families of different sibling compositions. *Child Development,* 1968, *39,* 1213-21.

Swift, J. N. Effects of early group experience: The nursery school and day nursery. In M. L. Hoffman and L. W. Hoffman (eds.), *Review of child development research.* Vol. I. New York: Russell Sage Foundation, 1964.

Talbot, N. B. Has psychologic malnutrition taken the place of rickets and scurvy in contemporary pediatric practice? *Pediatrics,* 1963, *31,* 909-18.

Terman, L. M., and Tyler, L. E. Psychological sex differences. In L. Carmichael (ed.), *Manual of child psychology.* New York: Wiley, 1954.

Thomas, A.; Chess, S.; and Birch, H. The origin of personality. In R. Atkinson (ed.), *Contemporary psychology.* San Francisco: Freeman, 1971.

Thomas, A.; Chess, S.; and Hertzig, M. E. A longitudinal study of primary reaction patterns in children. *Comprehensive Psychiatry,* 1960, *1,* 103-12.

Thompson, S. K. Gender labels and early sex role development. *Child Development,* 1975, *46,* 339.

Toman, W. *Family constellation.* New York: Springer, 1969.

Wessel, M. A., and La Camera, R. G. Care by parent: Further advantages. *Pediatrics,* 1969, *44,* 303-4.

White, B. L. An analysis of excellent early educational practices. *Interchange,* 1971, *2,* 71-88.

Williams, C. D. The elimination of tantrum behavior by extinction procedures. *Journal of Abnormal and Social Psychology,* 1959, *59,* 269.

Winnicott, D. W. Transitional objects and transitional phenomena. *International Journal of Psychoanalysis,* 1953, *34,* 89.

Wolff, P. H. The natural history of crying and other vocalizations in early infancy. In B. Foss (ed.), *Determinants of infant behavior.* Vol. IV. London: Methuen, 1970.

Wright, L.; Woodcock, J. M.; and Scott, R. Conditioning children when refusal of oral medication is life-threatening. *Pediatrics,* 1969, *44,* 969-72.

Yahraes, H. The effects of early experience on a child's development. *Mental Health Program Reports, 1968, 2.* Public Health Service Publication No. 1743.

Yarrow, L. J. The relationship between nutritive sucking experiences in infancy and non-nutritive sucking in childhood. *Journal of Genetic Psychology,* 1954, *84,* 149-62.

Yarrow, L. J. Separation from parents during early childhood. In M. L. Hoffman and L. W. Hoffman (eds.), *Review of child development research.* Vol. I. New York: Russell Sage Foundation, 1964.

Yawkey, T. D., and Griffith, D. L. The effects of the Premack principle on affective behaviors of young children. *Child Study Journal,* 1974, *4,* 59.

Zelazo, P. R.; Zelazo, N. A.; and Kolb, S. "Walking" in the newborn. *Science,* 1972, *176,* 314-15.

Zuger, B., and Taylor, P. Effeminate behavior present in boys from early childhood. II. Comparison with similar symptoms in non-effeminate boys. *Pediatrics,* 1969, *44,* 375-80.

Index